DUARTE CHRONICLES

CLAUDIA HELLER

Photography by Alan Heller

THE History PRESS

Published by The History Press
Charleston, SC 29403
www.historypress.net

All photos by Alan Heller unless otherwise noted.

First published 2013

Manufactured in the United States

ISBN 978.1.60949.882.5

Library of Congress CIP data applied for.

Notice: The information in this book is true and complete to the best of our knowledge. It is offered without guarantee on the part of the author or The History Press. The author and The History Press disclaim all liability in connection with the use of this book.

In loving memory of Beau Garrett Heller

CONTENTS

Five-term mayor Margaret Finlay has championed many causes over the years that have resulted in the envied quality of life Duarte residents enjoy. She is a tireless volunteer promoting education, environmental issues and Duarte's status in the San Gabriel Valley and beyond. *Courtesy of the City of Duarte.*

FOREWORD

As a member of a family that has had four generations living in Duarte for the last several decades with grandparents who settled here in the San Gabriel Valley in the 1930s, I know that once people live in Duarte, they always consider it home. Maybe it's the proximity to the base of our beautiful San Gabriel Mountains, or maybe it's the people who moved here and have created their lives here for generations. Then again, maybe it's the willingness by so many to serve their neighborhoods so selflessly. Whatever the reasons, you will find in the pages of this book a cast of characters as fascinating and eclectic as any heroes in our country's history.

Having served as mayor of Duarte for five terms, I have traveled the Los Angeles area for many years meeting thousands of people. These Southern Californians have read Claudia's accounts of Duarte life and lifestyles in the newspaper. Almost without exception, they remark that Duarte has had more than its share of colorful characters, historic adventures and dynamic conditions that have proved again and again the verity of the popular phrase that reverberates through our community: "Duarte Is Our Kind of Town." Prepare to be touched and taught by these intriguing vignettes that Claudia has so lovingly written. Duarte is a place, but the people truly make it my home.

MARGARET FINLAY
Mayor of Duarte

ACKNOWLEDGEMENTS

My thanks to the good people of Duarte who always step up when I need information or leads. The city staff, city council, school board and many service organizations and specialty clubs have always been there to help.

Over the years, many "old-time" Duarteans have shared their stories about the events that have shaped our community. These memories remain alive in the interviews they have granted.

Duarte's historical and contemporary events are captured on film by the staff at DCTV, Duarte's Public Access Channel, and the many shows produced by Mary Somerlott and the Reverend Neal Earle. Station Manager Levon Y, with his trusty camera and ROP student crew, has documented Duarte events for years and shared them with the public on television and online.

Living quietly on a ranch in the Siskiyou County town of Happy Camp, my sister, Karen Garrett, graciously proofed this book for me, and for that I am indebted.

The San Gabriel Valley Newspaper Group has printed my columns since 1991, allowing me to share with my readers about the people, events, wildlife and history of our community on a biweekly basis.

Special thanks to those who possess a keen memory of Duarte's history and are always there to share. Among them are Bill and Nita Norgard, Bruce and Mariellen Staller, Irwin Margiloff, Mark and Pauline Montgomery, Jack Collins and Jim Kirchner. And, of course, historian Steve Baker is always quick to share his vast knowledge of local history.

Birder extraordinaire Kimball Garrett, ornithologist and collections manager at the Los Angeles County Museum of Natural History, has led numerous expeditions along the San Gabriel River and adjacent lands, volunteering his time and expertise to educate the public about the natural history of the Duarte area. His skill has been invaluable, and my thanks go to him—thanks Bro!

Finally, a heap of gratitude goes to The History Press for recognizing the value of preserving local history, not only ancient history but also contemporary events and the people who are presently making history.

INTRODUCTION

Who am I to write about Duarte? Growing up under the "D" in the Hollywood sign with Griffith Park as my backyard, I had never heard of the town. Two miles up into Beachwood Canyon, my childhood home seemed worlds away from civilization, although I often walked to Hollywood High School, strolling along the famed Hollywood Boulevard. "The Valley" to me was the San Fernando Valley, and the existence of the San Gabriel Valley eluded me. It wasn't until 1980, when I moved to Duarte with my husband and three small children, that I discovered the beautiful San Gabriel Valley.

When we settled in a town of which we had never heard, little did we know that near the end of that year, Duarte would suffer one of its biggest disasters.

Soon we heard about Fish Canyon Falls, located in the canyon behind our neighborhood, and the City of Hope, which had worldwide recognition. We fell in love with the foothills to our north and the San Gabriel River to our east. Quite quickly, this valley became "The Valley," and the San Fernando Valley took on the role of the "Other Valley." In those early years, there remained some citrus orchards and avocado fields, acreage soon to be filled with homes and townhouses, all loosely straddling the main street, the Mother Road, Route 66.

Getting to Know Duarte

A first on our list was a visit to the Duarte Historical Museum, which at the time was located in a trailer in Duarte Park. Since that time, the patch

The original Duarte Historical Museum was lost in a land trade. Above is the structure that currently serves as the Duarte Historical Museum in Encanto Park, which was once the home of Buron Rogers Fitts (March 22, 1895–March 29, 1973), who served as the ninety-seventh lieutenant governor of California and later as a Los Angeles County district attorney. The house was located on the corner of Royal Oaks Drive and Cotter and was moved to Encanto Park when the Church of Jesus Christ of Latter Day Saints purchased the original property in order to build its church.

of land where the museum was located has become the subject of a trade and is now occupied by car dealerships. On our visit, the trailer door was locked, but after a few knocks, the docent invited us in. She was none other than Victoria Duarte Cordova, the great-great-granddaughter of Andres Duarte, the town's namesake. Cheerful and animated, she asked us to call her Vicki.

Vicki took us through the exhibits, explaining about the Gabrielino Indians, a name in reference to the Mission San Gabriel Arcangel located west of Duarte that was established by Spanish colonists in 1771. "The Native Americans were happy on this land," she said. "They had the mountains, the river and the fertile soil."

She moved on, telling us (with just a hint of pride) about Andres Avelino Duarte, born on November 30, 1805, one of twelve children born to Leandro and Maria Briones Duarte. She explained how he had joined the Mexican army at the age of sixteen, eventually serving as a mayordomo while stationed at the San Gabriel Mission. His assignment was to patrol the mission lands as far as San Bernardino. He was, as a young student once suggested to me, the historical version of a "neighborhood watch captain." Upon retirement in 1841, he petitioned Governor Juan Alvarado in Monterey for and received nearly seven thousand acres of land to call his own, which came to be known as Rancho Azusa de Duarte. Several cities have been established on lands originally granted to Andres Duarte. Other cities located on the rancho are Monrovia, Azusa, Irwindale, Baldwin Park, Arcadia and Bradbury.

Speaking of her ancestor, Vicki said he was content living on the land he loved, raising cattle and riding his horse below the foothills and along the Rio Azusa, now known as the San Gabriel River. His wife, Gertrudes, and their son Felipe Santiago Duarte (1828–1863) worked hard but enjoyed a peaceful life. Their home was built of adobe, a structure that is all but gone, with only a small part of it remaining in the pantry of a new home on the site. But times changed, and after the Mexican-American War (1846–48), Andres's dream began to turn into a nightmare. He was asked to prove that he owned the land, and that he did with his duly registered land grant. But he was then hit for "back taxes," and that spelled his doom. He and Gertrudes sold off portions of their land, the earliest transaction dating to 1855. By the early 1860s, they were in serious financial trouble, and the rancho was sold at auction to William Wolfskill in 1862.

Vicki was philosophical about the story but went on to show us more of the exhibits. She then pointed to the extensive citrus exhibit, which featured photos, crates, framed colorful and artistic labels and rusty smudge pots. She said that Duarte's climate and fertile soil were perfect for the growing of citrus and that with the subdividing of the rancho, citrus ranches then dominated the land. Oranges, lemons and avocados were the main crops, and the industry grew with the building of packinghouses. Horse-drawn carts would carry the crates loaded with fragrant citrus to the railroad for delivery to citrus-poor areas.

The museum then, as it does today, featured displays depicting the development of the citrus industry, the rise and fall of the ranchos, pioneer families and visionaries, artifacts from the Duarte family and various other historical exhibits.

By the end of our first year in Duarte, we were settled in. And then, on an otherwise unremarkable December day, a spark ignited the chaparral above Azusa, giving birth to a torrent of flames that deceptively gave little hint of marching west. As we retired that night, we could see light from the blaze to our east but were relieved that it remained far from our Duarte home and that the wind was blowing in an easterly direction.

Awoken at 1:00 a.m., we could hear fire engines and people talking in the street. The fickle winds had abruptly reversed direction, fanning the now-giant blaze to the west. The flames jumped the San Gabriel River and raced across the hillside above Duarte's foothill neighborhoods. Frenzied neighbors began watering down their homes and yards. Ash rained over as fire-borne winds roared down the canyon carrying embers that sparked small fires here and there. An eerie glow lit the early morning sky, as flames seemed to reach higher and higher on their westerly journey. And then, as fast as the fire had descended on our neighborhood, it grew suddenly quiet, and the wind ceased. "It must be out," I said foolishly. But no—it had merely passed through, and its wrath was now thundering west, devouring nearly forty homes on the Duarte Mesa before continuing on. Neighbors gathered on the street, relieved that their homes still stood. One neighbor, Mary Sutorius, ran into her home to bake cookies for the firemen. Residents farther down my street inspected burns on their roofs. And as we said silent words of relief, we had yet to learn of the devastation to those homes on the Duarte Mesa to our west.

The land on which Duarte is built is called alluvium, borne of sediment washed down from the San Gabriel Mountains. Historically, the area has been referred to as Upper and Lower Duarte, a phrase describing the topography, not the demographics. However, from the early days, the farm workers, the people of color and the poor had been relegated to "Lower Duarte," later known as "Rock Town," populating the land below Route 66 (Huntington Drive). Ranchers, who often lived in grand houses, occupied the foothill acreage. This division has always been a dividing point, although since the city's incorporation in 1957, many steps have been taken to rectify that perception.

Joining in the Community

After living in Duarte for several years, we became immersed in its social life. I joined the Duarte Woman's Club and found myself surrounded with women who selflessly volunteered their time to make Duarte a great place to live. In a weak moment, I volunteered to serve as block captain for the neighborhood watch program and for years served as editor and reporter of the monthly newsletter. I joined the Duarte Historical Society and studied the area's history. In time, I was asked to write a biweekly column for the

Pasadena Star News and thus became even more involved. People would ask, "How do you know what to write about?" I assured them that the biggest problem was to decide which story to write about. With every resident, there is a story. Our rich history boils over with tales to be told, factual and mythical events that envelop our past and the saga of those visionaries who gave us the quality of life we enjoy today.

There are stories about the Great Flood of 1938, stories of families who endured hardships but managed to eke out a good life in this town and stories of the rise and fall of the Red Cars. There are stories about local wildlife, the discovery of gold in our hills and the families who built cabins in Fish Canyon only to lose them to fire and flood. There are the highlights resulting in worldwide recognition, such as the Duarte Rotary admitting a woman and emerging as the successful party in a Supreme Court case. Like towns around us there is political Duarte, with signs sprouting up like spring flowers when an election is scheduled. There are those who work to make the town a better place to live and those reactionaries who mainly complain. It was researching, interviewing and writing these stories that gave me the insight to write this book. These pages are a compilation of a few of the columns that have appeared under my name in the local newspaper. Although the paper has changed names over the years, it is today part of the San Gabriel Valley Newspaper Group. The columns generally are not news stories but rather personal interest accounts about this town's past and present. From them, a visitor to our town might come to more intimately know what makes Duarte tick. Reviewing the articles for this book, I realized that despite the many years of writing columns, there are aspects of Duarte that are missing, a slight I intend to rectify in future columns.

Chapter 1

HISTORY

Lake Duarte Among Many City Sights

January 15, 2012

Within Duarte's borders, there are a number of historical sites overlooked by many residents, including "old-timers." Here are just a few:

The Hanging Tree: There are tales of swift justice carried out within our borders in the late 1800s. It is said that the oak tree located in the front courtyard of 1836–1806 Huntington Drive, just east of the 7-Eleven, was employed for this purpose.

Lake Duarte: Maybe better described as "Pond Duarte," this delightful body of water is located at the northern border of Royal Oaks Retirement Home at 1763 Royal Oaks Drive. Dozens of ducks paddle between its royal oaks–lined shore. Reportedly, the ducks visit daily, returning to Whittier Narrows each evening. Residents plant and maintain a flower and vegetable garden on the lake's southern bank.

Glenn Miller Park: At the top of Melcanyon Avenue in Fish Canyon sits a small park originally named Valley View Satellite Park. In 2001, music played by the Brass Quintet of the Air National Guard Band of the Southwest entertained at ceremonies honoring big-band leader Glenn Miller, whose home

Left: Among old Duarte tales is that of the "hanging tree," which purportedly facilitated swift justice during the town's rough and ready years in the late 1800s. The tree stands today in a courtyard on the south side of Huntington Drive just east of Highland.

Below: An appropriate sign marks Glenn Miller Park at the top of Melcanyon behind Valley View School. The park sits just a few dozen yards east of where the Miller Ranch was located before it burned down in 1980.

was once located just west of the park boundary. Miller, not yet forty years of age and enjoying the spotlight of the music world, organized the 418th Army Air Forces Band to support the U.S. troops fighting in World War II. Sadly, his plane vanished over the English Channel, ending his life. A bronze plaque sponsored by Truman Fisher, now deceased, and crafted by sculptor Richard Myer of Glendora was erected in the park by the Duarte Historical Museum. Soon after the plaque was dedicated, the Duarte City Council renamed the park Glenn Miller Park. The home Miller had built burned down in 1980.

Gaslights on the Mesa: Duarte is home to more than two thousand streetlights. Many are of the city-owned mission bell variety, while others are called "headlights" and are owned by Edison. However, as part of our community's heritage, there remain a handful of old gas lamps that illuminate the Duarte Mesa. These lights burn constantly, eliminating the need for a lamplighter to physically turn off the gas at dawn and light the flame each evening. Years ago, the Duarte Mesa Homeowners Association opted to pay for the gas rather than allow these historic and romantic lights to be replaced.

Cinco Robles: A song entitled "Cinco Robles," popular in the 1950s, was written by Larry Sullivan. It is said that he wrote the tune after spotting the street sign in Duarte. That sign was located on Duarte Road just west of the City of Hope. At this time, no sign at all marks Cinco Robles at Duarte Road, but the old street sign is on display at the Duarte Historical Museum. This sign is at the heart of a previously forgotten event in Duarte's history, one that will come to light in detail later in this book.

These are but a few of the unique gems hidden in plain sight around Duarte. They represent our distinctive heritage and may be visited by anyone out for an in-town adventure.

Remembering Rock Town: Residents Plan Reunion

August 9, 2007

Dig a hole in Duarte and you will discover that our community rests on alluvium. Giant boulders down to minute sand particles support our town, a fact largely unnoticed until we try to break ground. Perhaps this is why a

Douglas Ross remembers fondly his years living in Duarte's so-called Rock Town. During the 1960s, it was inhabited mostly by African American and Mexican working-class families. The construction of the 210 Freeway cut through its heart.

portion of Duarte was once known as "Rock Town," a term regarded by residents of the "Davis Addition" as one of affection rather than disrespect.

It was in the mid-1880s that a developer named Charles C. Davis subdivided a piece of rancho land in the southeastern portion of Duarte, hoping to start a new settlement. But with the collapse of the land boom, interest waned, and soon the area offered an opportunity for low-income workers to buy or build their homes on inexpensive land.

Once covering a large area, Rock Town borders shriveled when a large portion of the property south of the railroad tracks was bought by the government in the 1930s and later converted into the Santa Fe Dam site. But the heart of this settlement, inhabited by predominantly African American and Mexican working-class families, was a true community where everyone knew everyone else.

Douglas Ross, sixty, looks back fondly on his childhood in Rock Town. "It is where I spent my formative years," he says, "that land south of Huntington, north of Duarte Road, east of Highland and west of the river." Rocks dominate his memories. "We dodged rocks tumbling down the streets during the rainy season. We threw rocks in the river, and the homes had rock roofs," he recalls.

Historian Steve Baker describes Rock Town as a community within itself. The streets were loosely alphabetical: Berry, Cactus, Date, Elder, Filbert and Grape. As described in the book *On the Duarte*, the surrounding countryside was "acre after acre and row after row of orange and lemon groves, interrupted only by isolated ranch homes." Rock Town residents left their homes in the morning for work or school, many walking to catch the Red Car located two miles north on Royal Oaks Drive.

Students attended the Davis Addition School, which started at the first grade. For high school, they traveled to Monrovia to the Monrovia-Arcadia-Duarte High School called "MAD." Rock Town residents enjoyed their neighborhood stores and churches. "We walked everywhere, often barefoot," says Ross. "We would walk or take the Red Car to Monrovia to go to the Lyric Theater or the Monrovia Plunge."

The Ross family lived in a portion of the home of a Mr. Ford, who owned the grocery store on the corner of Filbert and Santo Domingo. Ross remembers clearly a day in 1951 when he was about four years old and wandered into Mr. Ford's store. "Just inside the door was a dead pig, on its back, legs in the air. A tub of blood was next to it. I dropped my money, turned around and ran." He describes a rural area, where he was in charge of the family's rabbits and chickens and his dad would milk the cows each night after returning home from his construction job.

Life in Rock Town changed dramatically when the 210 Freeway sliced through its heart. "Some residents were very happy," says Ross. "They received more money for their property than they ever expected to see." But Ross was devastated: "I was so angry and upset that this big freeway was going to divide our community."

So passionate about their memories of Rock Town, many former residents of the area have planned a reunion picnic they call the "Legacy of the Davis Addition: Rock Town 1884–1978." During the gathering, memorabilia from Rock Town's heyday will be on display at the Duarte Historical Museum, which is located in the park.

ELEGY FOR THE CHAPEL INN

July 21, 2011

Once a house of worship and later a steak house, Duarte's Chapel Inn is a part of Duarte history that lives on in the memories of longtime residents. It was located on what is now the west side of Highland Avenue, north of Huntington Drive (Route 66) and just south of the current fire station.

Originally a house of worship, the Chapel Inn later became a steak house. Built in 1898, the stained-glass windows were shipped from England around the Horn. Today, this church-turned-restaurant remains only in the memory of those who were once regular customers. *Courtesy of the Duarte Historical Museum.*

A group of English ranchers deeded land to Junius Maddock for the building of a mission, and in 1896, the cornerstone for the All Saints Episcopal Church was consecrated by the hierarchy of the Episcopal Diocese of Los Angeles. Following the dedication, the parishioners spent Sundays working for the church. After services, they would drive their wagons to the river to collect rocks for the walls of the church, building the little Norman Chapel.

Stained-glass windows for the church were shipped from England around the Horn and arrived in Duarte "without a crack," according to the book *On the Duarte.* The first services were held on January 6, 1898, officiated by Bishop Johnson before a congregation of parishioners from Duarte and Monrovia.

After St. Luke's Episcopal Church was opened in Monrovia, the congregation at All Saints dwindled down to six families. In 1926, the church was deconsecrated and resurrected as a restaurant.

The structure was purchased by Clarence and Delia Gordon and became a restaurant renowned throughout Southern California. Appropriately naming it the Chapel Inn, they preserved the church atmosphere and out of respect prohibited alcohol to be sold within its walls. Clarence, an accomplished carpenter, crafted the furniture for the inn using old pews for special tables. Dinners, served by candlelight, cost $2.75; lunches were $1.75. The regular menu consisted of steamed, battered and deep-fried chicken; mashed potatoes and gravy; a vegetable; and salad. Hot biscuits and homemade pies were served.

It is said that many famed stars graced the restaurant, including Claudette Colbert, Jean Harlow, Mary Pickford and Bette Davis. When the Gordons moved to Oregon, they sold the establishment to Annie Parsons of Pasadena. She carried on the tradition of excellence until World War II, when personal issues led her to sell the building to the Duarte post of the American Legion.

In time, the legion ran into financial difficulties and, in an effort to raise funds, held a raffle in 1963. The winner of one of the prizes was Isabel Zelasko, who won a beautiful unsigned painting of the Chapel Inn by artist George Dickenson. Isabel hung the painting at her residence, where it remained until recently, when she moved into Leven Oaks. Her friend and agent Odette Cuccaro, a charter member of Duarte American Legion Post 830, graciously donated the painting on her behalf to the Duarte Historical Museum, where it is now on display.

This story is now approaching its sad ending. Sold by the post, the building was bought by another entity that ran into trouble meeting tax obligations. In the end, and to the dismay of the community, the building was destroyed. History-minded residents swore to see that such a thing would never happen again to Duarte's historical buildings. However, since that time, Duarte has seen many of its historical icons vanish, including the Evergreen Motel, the Trails Restaurant, the Blvd. Cafe, the Big Sky Drive In and the Columbia Bowl.

The original altar of the All Saints Church is on display in the Chapel Room at the Duarte Museum. It is covered with an altar cloth from the San Gabriel Mission, donated by the late Victoria Duarte Cordova, the great-great-granddaughter of Andres Duarte.

Evergreen Motel: A Mother Road Icon

December 28, 2006

Duarte's modest stretch of Route 66 developed much like the rest of the Mother Road. As travelers braved the distances, a need for services grew, and enterprising families opened their doors to overnighters, serving warm meals in their kitchens.

This Mission-style house was designed by architect John C. Austin and built in 1910 for Elmer B. Radabaugh and his family. It later became a sanatorium and then a motel. Located on Duarte's Route 66, the Evergreen Motel was razed in 2007 despite its historical significance.

Eventually, a variety of motels beckoned weary motorists, vying for their business with colorful neon signs, while burger stands like the Blvd. Cafe thrived.

Duarte was no exception. Dozens of motels sprung up along Huntington Drive, flanked by food stands, cafés and roadside vendors. Vacationers, families moving from east to west and wannabe stars heading for Hollywood enjoyed the comforts and hospitality of the mom-and-pop motels and stores.

But travelers are a fickle lot. With the official decommissioning of Route 66 in 1985, Burma Shave signs were but a memory as travelers opted for the speedier route, abandoning the Mother Road for interstate highways. Locally, Route 66 was no match for the Foothill (210) Freeway, and the flurry of motel patrons dwindled as fast as they had appeared. There was, of course, still a market for overnight accommodations and restaurants, but with travel time reduced, the abundance of motels was overkill. Establishments that could not compete were left eerily vacant, and many fell into disrepair. One motel that remains today is the Evergreen, just east of City Hall on the south side of Huntington Drive.

The Mission-style house designed by architect John C. Austin was built in 1910 for Elmer B. Radabaugh and his family, according to Irwin Margiloff, curator of the Duarte Historical Museum. The house was occupied by the Radabaugh family until the late 1930s, after which it became a sanatorium and, later, a motel with additional rooms in separate structures built at the rear of the property.

"The house's history was brought to light when Jim Schibanoff, a Del Mar physician, was researching the Austin-designed Canfield-Wright house in Del Mar and found reference to a house in Duarte built in Mission style with certain features," Margiloff said. After some research and the help of historian Steve Baker, it was discovered that the Evergreen Motel was that house.

Austin was chief architect of the Los Angeles City Hall, the Griffith Observatory and the Shrine Auditorium. Another of Austin's works is the Carnegie Library building in Anaheim, which is now the Anaheim Museum.

Interestingly, before moving into the house that became the Evergreen Motel, the Radabaughs lived in a stick Victorian-style house built in 1896 that remains today on Vineyard Avenue in Duarte.

The Evergreen's future is precarious, as the site is earmarked for a new library.

Note: The Evergreen Motel was demolished in 2007 to make room for a new library. However, funds for a new library were never realized, and at the printing of this book, the lot remains vacant.

AIR TRAGEDY SHOWED DUARTE'S METTLE

March 8, 2007

It was 6:00 p.m. on a quiet Sunday evening when many Duarte families were enjoying time together before the start of another week. But the calm was short-lived, as windows rattled and homes shook, sending residents fleeing into the streets in a state of panic. What many assumed to be an earthquake proved to be the unimaginable. At 6:08 p.m. on June 6, 1971, an Air West DC-9 passenger plane and a Navy F-4 Phantom jet collided over Duarte. Bodies and debris rained from the sky over a square mile area of

Fish Canyon. All forty-eight persons aboard the DC-9 were killed. The navy jet pilot also perished, but a radar operator parachuted to safety.

The first frenzied moments of confusion and horror were followed by concern and action as the community united in aiding the rescue efforts. As crews of firefighters and rescue workers descended on this little town, businesses, civic organizations and individuals rallied to the cause. A few days following the crash, Duartean Louise Hewitt commented, "It was a terrible tragedy, but it has drawn together the men, women and children of all races and creeds in this community. I'm proud of Duarteans—we've come a long way."

Recovery efforts were headquartered at Royal Oaks Park, where eight helicopters from the U.S. Marine Corps were based between flights into the crash site about three miles away. Agencies such as the sheriff's department, the county fire department and rescue squads from neighboring communities organized while local folks supplied food and aid. The Duarte Youth Acres (DYA) chuck wagon was first to arrive at the command and immediately set up to serve meals. The Duarte Woman's Club, PTAs from local schools and a host of businesses including Thrifty's, Alpha Beta, the Pantry, Weber's Bread Company and Altadena Dairy brought sandwiches and coffee. The Duarte McDonald's restaurant donated hundreds of hamburgers for the rescue crews.

Students from Mount Olive High School and members of the Self Help Center ran errands and made deliveries for the workers. The Monrovia Fire Department responded to a request from the L.A. County Fire Department's Duarte Station 44 to set up an emergency lighting system.

Recovered bodies were flown to Royal Oaks Park by helicopter and immediately transferred to a van and taken directly to the coroner's office. Representatives of Air West remained at the command post, as did firefighters resting between shifts and investigators from Washington representing the National Transportation Safety Board. The crash and explosion sparked several fires, which resulted in substantial charring of the mountainous area.

The passenger plane was flying from Los Angeles to Salt Lake City, and the majority of crew and passengers was from the Seattle area.

As so eloquently stated by Hewitt, the event was tragic and weighed heavily on the minds of the local residents, but it is heartwarming to know that this small community can rally together in a time of need and work together for a common cause.

FORGOTTEN DUARTE HISTORY

December 2010

Murder, campus unrest, a city council member found guilty of shoplifting—these are a few of the events hiding in the closet of this town. Now, these and accounts of a more positive nature are available to the public in a series of scrapbooks containing newspaper clippings from 1947 through 1964.

She may have been obsessive about saving memorabilia, but Lucile Phillips Morrison's penchant for organizing and preserving just about everything that crossed her desk has provided historians today with a treasure of documented information about our local history. Recently, her grandson, Chris Morrison, donated a dozen scrapbooks compiled by Lucile to the Duarte Historical Society. The books had been preserved at the Phillips-Morrison Institute in Tiburon, California.

The Morrison family owned land on Huntington Drive since 1888, when Dr. Wayland Morrison's father bought the twenty-seven-acre site that included the land where the Amberwood Homes are located today. Eventually, the Morrisons donated part of the ranch to Westminster Gardens, allowing expansion of the retirement facility that, at the time, was reserved for retired missionaries of the United Presbyterian Church. Today, that facility is a retirement home without religious affiliation. Another portion of the ranch was donated to Duarte Youth Acres for a recreational and sports facility.

In addition to her hobby of documenting local history, Lucile was active in the city. It is said she was so active that she slept only a few hours a night in order to keep up with her busy life. She was the first president of the Duarte Community Service Council, which was organized to "coordinate, improve and add to the social human values of the community as a whole." That club is still active today. She published a best-selling novel entitled *The Lost Queen of Egypt* in 1937 and wrote extensively for the *Duarte Newsletter* from 1946 to 1953.

The scrapbooks she created cover many aspects of Duarte life during the early years and are carefully labeled. Among them are "Citizens" (1955–57), "Civil Defense" (1960–64), "Parks and Recreation" (1948–56 and 1956–60), "Women's Clubs" (1947–64) and "Incorporation" (1957–61). These news clippings give a comprehensive view of what life was like in Duarte and the events that transpired to shape our community into what it is today.

The "Crime and Tragedies" scrapbook sets forth a number of news articles from robberies, assaults and shootings to malicious mischief and reports of gang activity. In 1950, a nine-year-old boy died from head injuries following a one-hundred-foot fall into a gravel pit. One story appearing in 1954 alleges that the first bank robbery in Duarte occurred but then reveals that the robbery involved a piggy bank containing five dollars stolen from a Duarte home. In 1953, headlines included "Arrests Break Up Valley Heroin Ring" and "Boy Rescued in Reservoir by Neighbor."

One of Duarte's most scandalous stories involved the recall of city council member Vera Hacker in 1960. Hacker had been found guilty of petty theft and, following petition, was recalled by a "wide margin of Duarte voters."

DUARTE'S PAST LINGERS IN TOWN ON THE MOVE

February 23, 2002

Duarte is a town in which old and new blend in such subtle fashion that, even traveling through town, we experience the past, present and future.

Driving on Huntington Drive (Route 66), a variety of banners decorates the median. In the months ahead, watch for the colorful new banners that depict citrus crate labels, a subject representative of Duarte's past.

With the flair of Mary Barrow Somerlott's creative mind, coupled with Mark Wood's artistry, these labels may be viewed as decoration, but they also tell a story of those who came before us. Take John Scott for example. He and his wife, Sarah, came to Duarte from Canada in 1883, purchasing ninety-six acres of land that started at the foothills above Bradbourne Avenue and ended at Huntington Drive. Scott laid out orchards of prunes, peaches, apricots, plums, oranges and lemons. He also planted olives. He became the horticultural inspector of the Los Angeles County Agricultural Department. His goal was to protect California from pests carried on imported fruit.

A leader in the citrus industry, Duarte not only earned many prestigious awards, but employment was also high at the orchards and packinghouses. The oldest 4-H Club in Southern California was organized in Duarte in 1929, sponsored by the University of California Extension's Department of Agriculture.

The citrus label banners soon to appear will remind us every day of an important part of local history.

On the eastern end of town, we can look sadly to the north and lament the loss of the Trails Restaurant, where many of us had spent pleasant evenings. But on the south side of Huntington, we can see that the Elks Lodge is nearing completion. It promises to be the site of happy times for not only members but also the public.

As for our residents, there are those who are moving along in life. It was business as usual at a recent city council meeting when one man took the microphone to have his say. When he directed his comment to council member Tzeitel Paras, the audience woke up. "Will you marry me?" he asked of her.

Councilwoman Paras graduated from Duarte High School in 1989 and met her suitor, K.C. Caracci, while the two worked together. Several years later, they met again, but their friendship did not blossom into love until a few years ago, when Paras was campaigning for her council seat. "That was a trying time, but he weathered it," she said. An August wedding is planned.

A Glimpse into '50s Local Life

June 9, 2011

There was a time when Duarte's population had not yet exploded and a newspaper that was dedicated to what was going on around town existed. Even the most modest milestones made the headlines, and residents always knew who was doing what!

It was in April 1955 that a fundraiser was held to benefit a former Duarte resident, Jill Kinmont. A twenty-year-old ski champion, Jill was paralyzed in a ski accident. She had resided on Royal Oaks Drive with her family. She became a symbol of courage during her recovery efforts, and a movie was made about that journey. More than $3,000 was raised in the Duarte fundraising event.

Also in 1955, the residents of Duarte were invited to view the latest in entertainment—a color television! Wilson Radio & Sound, located on Huntington Drive, opened its doors for residents to watch the first color telecast of a Broadway musical.

A Duarte housewife that year won the "Queen for a Day" title. The mother of six children told the master of ceremonies, Jack Bailey, that the family had suffered a number of medical problems and there was no money

The *Duarte Dispatch*, part of Foothill Intercity Newspapers, claimed on its front-page banner to be the "Only Newspaper In The World That Gives a Darn About Duarte!" *Courtesy of the Duarte Historical Museum.*

even for necessities. The family was showered with gifts, including a vacation, household items, a freezer and shoes for the kids.

Also making headlines was Hans Sulzer's cow, Clara, which gave birth to triplet bull calves. Another story features photos and an article about a police chase that succeeded in roping a calf that had escaped from its pen. The ending was a sad one, however, as the animal was to die soon afterward from overexertion.

The *Duarte Dispatch*, part of Foothill Intercity Newspapers, claimed on its front-page banner to be the "Only Newspaper In The World That Gives a Darn About Duarte!" And it really did. Twice weekly, community events—no matter how small—were routinely covered. Local school sports dominated the sports page, to the delight of students and parents. But on July 26, 1992, all that changed. The final edition announced, "After more than seventy years of uninterrupted publication…the Foothill Intercity Newspapers will cease to exist. However, the communities of Arcadia, Temple City, Monrovia and Duarte will be served with the introduction of a daily newspaper for the entire region." Thus, the *Foothill Star Tribune* emerged.

What was happening around Duarte at the time of the paper's final edition? "Wienermobile On Its Way to Area." This article announced that the "Oscar Mayer Wienermobile, familiar to every child who has watched cartoons on TV, will be making some local pit stops in the next few days. The twenty-three-foot-long fiberglass wienie-wagon, which plays twenty-one versions of the Oscar Mayer jingle and spouts the steamy aroma of hotdogs, is easy to spot in any parking lot."

Local deaths, marriages and births warranted full stories and photos during those years, and anyone receiving an award was sure to receive full media coverage. Even home addresses were printed in the stories.

These newspaper articles reflect a more innocent time when neighbors seemed to have close-knit relationships and community pride was at an all-time high.

DUARTE REACHING HALF A CENTURY

December 28, 2006

Congratulations! Duarte is celebrating fifty years of incorporation this year, and this milestone is marked by a series of fun, educational and unifying celebrations. But let's turn back to 1962, when Duarte celebrated its fifth anniversary with a tour highlighting "points of interest in Duarte." The plan, conceived by the managing editor of *The Duartean* and carried out by the Duarte Chamber of Commerce, the Duarte Unified School District, the city staff and "civic minded citizens," consisted of two car caravans leaving City Hall, then situated on Third Street, and visiting such local sites as City of Hope, Columbia Ribbon & Carbon Co., Duarte Water Company, Wright Tract (Model Home), Hamburger Heaven, De Forest Pottery Company and Minneapolis Honeywell Corporation.

Local businesses celebrated the milestone date with large ads in the *Duartean*. Handy Dandy Department Store offered discounts such as shoes, shirts and gowns for $1. Royal Oaks Village (at the northeast corner of town) invited the public to visit its model homes and boasted "excitingly different homes in a select community priced from $19,500 to $19,950." And there were words of congratulations from a variety of merchants along Huntington Drive such as Camper's Haven, Rogers Donut Drive In, the Sho House, the Hawaiian Restaurant, the Colonial Pancake House, Crest Cleaners and Thompsons' Sleep Shop.

The "spirit of celebration" would be rekindled a few months later as the annual Duarte Days Fiesta consumed the community with a "gigantic parade, barbeque and dance." These were the days when the community was represented by Miss Duarte, and in 1964, Kathy McFarland, a Duarte High School senior, was chosen to reign. There was a youth parade led by grand marshal Rocky Shahan, star of the *Rawhide* TV series. The Duarte Falcon Band, the Falconettes, the Northview Junior Cardinal Band, the Cardettes Drill Team and Tammy Shanter Caledonian Pipe Band performed. The mayor at the time was William Lancaster.

The festivities continued on into the evening with a teen dance at City Hall featuring Eddie and the Showmen providing the music and Casey Kasem acting as emcee.

Ending the celebration was the much-anticipated drawing. Miss Duarte drew the winning ticket to match the one held by Dorothy Mink, who went home that night $1,000 richer. And so ended the Duarte Fiesta.

While news of the Fiesta Day events dominated the *Duartean* that day, a few other stories of interest appeared, such as the grand opening of the Duarte office of the Citizens for Goldwater-Miller Organization, the search by Edison for an "outstanding science student" who would be a "possible delegate to the National Youth Conference in Chicago" and the Duarte Falcons breaking their existing record of consecutive victories as they won their fourth straight game of the season, defeating the Sierra Vista Dons forty to seven.

Maddock Ranch to Become a Bed-and-Breakfast?

January 1995

When Junius and Agnes Maddock came to Duarte in 1883, little did they know that their eventual decision to build a home in the local foothills would create an issue for Duarteans in 1995.

The 1904 Queen Anne–style house is set on a high dressed granite foundation fashioned from stones from the San Gabriel River and boasts four tall brick chimneys. This imposing abode is modestly hidden from view, nestled in the midst of the Hearthstone Development, which flanks Las Lomas Drive above Royal Oaks Park.

Putting their home on the market, present owners Jim and Ardyce Stafford and their realtor, Carol Hinds of Foothills Real Estate Services, hope to preserve the historical house, realizing that it is located on prime

This 1904 Queen Anne–style house was the home of Junius and Agnes Maddock, who came to Duarte in 1883. Now surrounded by the Hearthstone development, the house once served as a bed-and-breakfast. It is presently a private home.

land for development. Their dreams for preserving what we call today the "Maddock Ranch" may be answered by John Tseng, who owns a bed-and-breakfast in Old Town Pasadena.

Tseng, who admits to "falling in love with the property," had proposed development plans that in no way would compromise the home, its beautiful landscaping and gazebo. These plans include a six-room bed-and-breakfast filled with period antiques, and he has applied to the city for a conditional use permit that would allow him to do so.

Over the next several weeks, public input, particularly from residents in the area, will be solicited and the matter considered by the Duarte Planning Commission.

Note: Tseng did indeed purchase the property, improve it while protecting the integrity of the house and then open a bed-and-breakfast. It was well received by guests, who filled the house, celebrating weddings and family reunions. But neighbors were quick to complain about parking and noise, and although the city attempted to negotiate a compromise, it was not to be. Sadly, Tseng gave up on the venture and sold the house. Today, it stands quietly owned by a private family.

Kellogg House: Artist Paints House's Colorful Past

November 27, 2008

There was once in Duarte an oasis of sorts—a compound largely ignored by the populace and hidden in the shade of a small forest, east of where the CVS store now stands. Known as the "Shelt'ring Wing," this quiet Christian Science convalescent home was doomed when the now busted real estate boom rendered it fodder to developers, forcing it to follow the fate of many local icons: demolished, divided and developed.

In the midst of this familiar story of loss there remains a bright spot: a gem known as the Kellogg House. The only remaining structure from the Shelt'ring Wing days, this circa 1930s home is surrounded by modern houses

Once part of a Christian Science convalescent home called the Shelt'ring Wing, the Kellogg House is all that remains of the compound and is privately owned. It once was the site of grand parties, where such celebrities as Glenn Miller reportedly frequented. The painting was created by *plein air* artist BJ Lane.

rather than a forest, but its colorful history envelops the structure, though it has been tastefully modernized and remodeled, leaving only a shadow of its previous state.

It is said that the Kellogg family (not related to the cereal branch) sold the house to the Christian Science Church and it became part of a compound promoting healing "through a spirit of love." The Shelt'ring Wing was later merged into the church's Broadview facility.

The remaining home, presently owned by Sean and Carol Siqueiros, boasts a colorful past with stories about such regular visitors as actor Clark Gable and famed big-band leader Glenn Miller. As Sean's father, Robert, gave me a tour of the home, I was impressed with the spacious rooms, the beige custom hand-painted cobblestone brick floor and the two sets of rounded bay windows that punctuate the custom look of the house. "Originally, this was the maid's room," said Robert, pointing out a small sitting room. "She had her own entrance."

The home contains five fireplaces and five bedrooms and is surrounded by gardens complete with a fountain. Gardening plots were cleared of vegetation. "I used to grow vegetables, but no one liked them, so I stopped," Robert explained. The backyard is definitely groomed for family gatherings, with a barbeque area, bar and plenty of room for children to play. The home was calm and as quiet as a library during my tour, but Robert assured me that the house is geared to family life and is traditionally brimming with rambunctious grandchildren and adult family members gathered around the large granite breakfast bar or running gleefully through the yard.

Over the main fireplace, a painting of the house is displayed. Drawn by the unique architecture, local *plein air* artist BJ Lane asked the owners if she could create a painting of the home. After deciding on the best angle, she went to work. The result was so stunning that the owners bought the painting and proudly display it. Thrilled to have created the lovely painting, artist Lane says:

> *Painting city architecture en plein air* [in the open air] *is one of my lifelong passions. Over the years, I have painted city scenes in Southern California, Arizona and Oregon and in several countries in Europe. Many times, I have discovered unique, historical places right here in my own hometown of Duarte.*
>
> *The Kellogg House was a joy to finally paint, as I had been looking for its location for a long time. It is tucked away within a newer housing tract, and one morning I discovered this beauty. The back of the house is splendid,*

and one can imagine the parties that were given in its time. But I felt the front of this house deserved recognition and chose the south entrance as my artistic perspective. I begin my paintings on location with a unique medium, oil bars [oil paint in a solid form], *and finish the pieces in my studio, adding the final details to the canvas with the help of reference photos taken at the scene. In this painting, begun November 2007, I added the Christmas decorations that the owners had placed in their yard as a final detail.*

THE YEAR 1913: CITY OF HOPE AND SANTA TERESITA

January 3, 2013

It looks like life is continuing despite threats of doom, and here we are at the year 2013. A century ago, in the year 1913, the world celebrated many milestones, and the news accounts are both humorous and prophetic.

On January 26, Jim Thorpe relinquished his 1912 Olympic medals for being a pro, and here, one hundred years later, we see Lance Armstrong stripped of his awards in light of doping charges. In May 1913, the British House of Commons rejected a woman's right to vote, while today we grapple with the legal right of gays to marry.

A good part of today's news is about taxes. It was on October 3, 1913, that the federal income tax became law at 1 percent and the Federal Reserve Act was signed. In the same month, President Woodrow Wilson said that the United States "will never attack another country."

Closer to home, it is said that two ragtag tents were erected near the San Gabriel River on the southeast corner of Duarte, giving birth to what we know today as a state-of-the-art, world-class biomedical research, treatment and education center. This year, the City of Hope celebrates its one-hundred-year existence.

While many people came to Duarte during the early part of the century to enjoy the local recreational opportunities, others came for their health. Although hunting, fishing and hiking in our foothills were draws, the mild temperature was a magnet for those suffering from asthma or tuberculosis. As a result, several sanitariums were built, probably the two most well known of which were the City of Hope and Santa Teresita.

When the City of Hope was founded by the Jewish Consumptive Relief Association, some locals were opposed to it, fearful that they would become

The Workingmen Circle No 248 building, dedicated on May 9, 1915, was typical of early housing for tuberculosis patients at the City of Hope. The structure was designed to maximize patients' access to fresh air and sunshine, which, along with rest and healthy food, was then considered the best treatment for the disease. *Courtesy of the City of Hope archives.*

infected with tuberculosis. The hospital's meager beginnings were fraught with obstacles, not the least of which was the constant flooding when the river breached its banks during the rainy season.

Santa Teresita opened several years later. It was in 1930 that the Carmelite Sisters of the Most Sacred Heart, who had fled religious persecution in Mexico, established the sanitarium to treat patients suffering from tuberculosis or, as they called it in those days, consumption. It later became an acute care hospital, expanding from its original three-acre plot. The rise and fall of this hospital includes the establishment of acute care and manor skilled nursing facilities. It was one of the first of its kind to use electronic records.

When a statewide nurse-patient ratio status was mandated, the hospital struggled to adhere and eventually closed.

In some ways, 1913 doesn't seem so long ago.

CITY'S NAMESAKE IS BACK ON THE RANCHO BUT NOT QUITE HOME

By Mary Barrow Somerlott
August 2007

Don Andres Avelino Duarte is coming closer to his monumental return home to the rancho he loved and ultimately lost. When he returns, he will be tall in the saddle, bronzed from his journey from China and "guaranteed [to remain so] for at least a thousand years," notes sculptor/artist Richard Myer, responsible for the original design used to create the fourteen-foot-high bronze of the city's namesake.

The statue of Andres Duarte depicted proudly atop his stallion was completed in late July at the foundry in Dalian, China, and shipped to Los Angeles in a container that could barely hold the massive piece that

The fourteen-foot-high statue of Andres Avelino Duarte on his stallion is the result of a community effort and pays tribute to the man for whom Duarte is named. It is located on Huntington Drive (Route 66) in a plaza across the street from City Hall. Once again, Duarte keeps watch over his rancho.

weighs more than two tons. Upon its arrival on August 9, the statue was transported to temporary accommodations at a large facility in Azusa for what city officials and the Duarte in Bronze committee of the Duarte Historical Society hope will be a short detour until plans can be worked out on a permanent site.

Originally, the statue was to be placed at the northeast corner of Huntington Drive and Mount Olive. But once the statue began taking on its larger-than-life size, it became apparent that the originally selected site was too small. The location had been decided at a time when a statue of Andres Duarte as a lone standing figure was being considered.

Now city officials are proposing that the statue be installed in a new community plaza that would be constructed on a nearly half-acre piece of city-owned land across the street from City Hall. The plaza was already on the drawing boards for the future, a concept of the Downtown Duarte Advisory Committee to the Duarte Economic Development Commission, to provide a gathering place for community events. Discussions are now underway to see if it is possible to move ahead on construction plans.

Note: The above article preceded the gala event featuring the statue unveiling and was written by Duarte's publicist, Mary Barrow Somerlott.

ANDRES DUARTE STATUE TOPS OFF A BIG YEAR

December 2007

The year 2007 has been a particularly exciting one for Duarte. Celebrating the fiftieth anniversary of the city's incorporation, various local organizations have sponsored events throughout the year to not only acknowledge the anniversary but also to educate and entertain residents.

The highlight of the year was the arrival of the fourteen-foot-tall bronze statue, an event eclipsed only by the exciting and overwhelming success of the dedication ceremonies at the statue plaza across the street from City Hall on Huntington Drive (Route 66).

Not only were nearly fifty members of the Duarte family present, some traveling from as far as Hawaii, but dignitaries from throughout Southern California also joined in the ceremonies. In all, it is estimated the cheering crowd numbered nearly five hundred.

At its dedication in 2007, more than fifty descendants of Andres Avelino Duarte traveled from throughout the United States to attend the unveiling of the statue. It is a tribute to Duarte's history and a symbol of community pride.

Even those who viewed the statue during its brief surprise appearance at the Salute to Route 66 Parade last month could not suppress an emotional "Ahhhh" as the covering was flung from the statue, revealing its bronzed glory in the afternoon sunlight.

It was a long journey for Andres Duarte, beginning with the fundraising efforts of the Duarte Historical Society, the creative artwork of sculptor Richard Myer, the creation of the actual statue at a foundry in China and then the sea voyage, with Duarte's head protruding from the shipping container. The statue is believed to be the first bronze statue erected on Route 66 in honor of an early California land grant holder.

The dream was to have something unique to Duarte's heritage—not just a statue but also a symbol of community pride. Sadly, Victoria Duarte Cordova, great-great-granddaughter of Andres Duarte, did not live to see the finished statue, although she had served on the statue committee for several months.

The unveiling and dedication included presentations by federal, state and county officials, followed by a dinner held for the Duarte family at the Ranchero Mexican Restaurant, hosted by the Duarte Historical Society.

MEMORIES ARE MADE OF THIS: A JUKEBOX SHOP

October 23, 1996

A variety of treasures hides behind a door at an unlikely spot along Huntington Drive, Duarte's little stretch of Route 66. Open that door and step into a nostalgic world of massive wood-and-plastic monsters that stand silently among car banks, signs and oilcans. Drop a quarter into the slot and pick a song title and the room fills with memories of rollicking times gone by.

Jukebox Memories, owned and operated by Merle Nottingham, is one of Duarte's best-kept secrets. A resident of Duarte since 1970, Nottingham once worked in the furniture refinishing business. He occasionally restored jukebox cabinets, and curiosity led him to tinker with their inner workings. Eventually, he gained a worldwide reputation for jukebox repair and opened up shop in his garage. When his jukebox collection finally outgrew its space, he opened Jukebox Memories in 1986. Known for his quality service, maintenance and acquisition of jukeboxes, Nottingham counts some impressive names among his clients: Danny DeVito, Katherine Helmond,

Jukebox Memories, owned and operated by Merle Nottingham, was one of Duarte's best-kept secrets. Behind those doors, nostalgia reigned. It is yet another Route 66 icon that has vanished.

Burt Reynolds and many producers and songwriters. At this time, he owns about ten jukeboxes, a slim down from previous days, when nearly twenty-five of these music machines adorned his shop.

"They're getting hard to find," states Nottingham, noting that his collection mainly consists of 1940s and 1950s versions. He notes that eight- and forty-five-rpm records are easy to find at flea markets and that forty-five-rpm records are still being made for modern jukeboxes. "Many people collect for nostalgic reasons," he states, "and 1950s diners have become very popular. These antique remote controls allow diner patrons to be booth potatoes while playing the jukebox."

A 1900 Mutoscope complete with Charlie Chaplin flicks sits among his collection, and for a penny, you can operate the hand crank that rotates cards on a reel. Antique oil cans and car banks line the walls, adding to the nostalgic aura that permeates the shop.

Note: Jukebox Memories is now just a memory.

ROWDY, VISITED BY ROYALTY

August 7, 2008

A "wild mêlée" in Duarte? A visit by royalty? This may not sound like the quiet Duarte we know today, but there was a time…

Swiss Park

When Swiss Park was razed in the late 1980s, more than a Route 66 icon was lost. It all began when seven acres were purchased in 1947 "in order to provide a home for an active and growing Swiss community in the Los Angeles area." At the time, the acreage was brush- and rock-covered land surrounded by orange groves, typical of the day. Following two years of mostly volunteer work, Swiss Park, 2501 East Huntington Drive, blossomed into a garden spot with chalet-type buildings and facilities for banquets.

Swiss Park eventually became open to the public for rental.

Although family gatherings and banquets sponsored by community organizations were the norm, it was the week before Labor Day in 1958 when thousands of sheet-metal workers descended on the Swiss Park Pavilion, which they had rented for a party. Reportedly, there were six special deputies on duty at the site, which did not seem to deter the event from escalating into a fracas that spilled into the surrounding neighborhoods, causing residents to turn on their sprinklers to keep partygoers off their lawns.

The city council meeting that followed was attended by fifty irate citizens who complained that "their good natures were ruffled by the three-day mêlée" and that they were worried that a repeat of the out-of-control activities might occur during the upcoming three-day weekend. As it turned out, the unfortunate experience was not repeated, and Swiss Park was the scene of many events, both peaceful and memorable.

Swiss Park is now located in Whittier.

Royal Visit

Where WePackItAll stands today, at the corner of Encanto Parkway (then called Fish Canyon Road) and Huntington Drive, is a building that was

A plaque commemorating a visit by the Earl of Snowdon, then husband of Her Royal Highness Princess Margaret, on November 9, 1965, was placed on a building that is now home to WePackItAll. The royal appearance celebrated the opening of Johnson Motors, Inc., the distributor for Triumph and BSA motorcycles.

once occupied by Johnson Motors, Inc., the distributor for Triumph and BSA motorcycles. On November 9, 1965, the Earl of Snowdon, husband of Her Royal Highness Princess Margaret, officially dedicated the new headquarters, which was completed the following year. Several hundred spectators gathered at the dedication ceremony.

Newspaper articles describing the event reported that Lord Snowdon's appearance was evidence of "the importance of motorcycle manufacturing to British trade as well as his own interest in the two-wheeled sport."

It was here that British-made motorcycles were distributed throughout the United States. Eventually, this enterprise moved on, and the once-celebrated building fell into disrepair until purchased by WePackItAll, which has renovated the area. Memories of the visit by British royalty have all but faded, with one reminder that marks the spot, a plaque that reads: "This building officially dedicated by the Earl of Snowdon, November 9, 1965, A.D."

For Duarteans, the Bells Toll

April 17, 2005

For years, Duarteans have celebrated the Mother Road, promoting our little stretch of Route 66. But there is another famous celebrated road along Huntington, and that is the El Camino Real. Although our main street is not a part of the King's Highway, we are a part of its rich history, and our proximity to the San Gabriel Mission and the legacy of our city's namesake, Andres Duarte, links us with that historic byway.

The mission bells on the median along Huntington Drive are an example of our city's recognition of a historic era in which the California missions were established, from the first (San Diego, 1769) to the last (present-day Sonoma, 1823), built mainly in areas where large populations of Indians lived. Of course, over the years, the dusty road was replaced by highways, but the almost mystic aura of that period has endured.

Many organizations over the years have made an effort to preserve the El Camino Real and place markers along its route. As far back as 1892, the California Federation of Women's Clubs (CFWC), with which our own Duarte Woman's Club is affiliated, was instrumental in forming the El Camino Real Association. The goal was to create a marker that resembled

The mission bells on the median along Huntington Drive are an example of our city's recognition of a historic era during which the California missions were established. This theme is evident throughout the city.

a cast-iron bell hung from a bent guidepost. The first was placed in 1906 in front of the Old Plaza Church in Los Angeles. Although 158 bells were installed by 1915, time, weather, vandalism, road construction and theft took a toll.

Today, through a grant, Caltrans is restoring the mission bell marker system, with one bell every two miles from San Francisco through Orange County. These bells were cast from a mold made from one of the original bells installed before 1920. As guardian of the bells, Caltrans is responsible for their upkeep and replacement. The project continues to be supported by the CFWC, as well as other community service organizations. There is also a program in place wherein individuals may adopt a bell to care for.

Duarte also pays tribute to the mission era with bell-shaped streetlights. They can be seen along Encanto Parkway, and a few, such as on Royal Oaks near Cotter and two on Buena Vista, are placed elsewhere in town. The balance of the streetlights in town display the "cobra head" design and are maintained by Edison. The mission bell–style lights are maintained by the city.

Nothing Left but Memories for the Trails

September 23, 2001

"Sentimental journey" read the sign near the door as I entered a dimly lit Trails Restaurant House and Bar in the midst of an auction bent on shedding all that had served the Route 66 icon well since the early 1950s.

The sign summed up the history of the lounge and restaurant that once offered hearty meals to motorists along the Mother Road and had managed to survive long after the freeway lured travelers from the celebrated highway.

Earlier this year, we had sipped gin and tonics in the lounge area as we were entertained by the regulars huddling at the bar and the gang socializing around the organ. We chatted with the seasoned waitress and devoured the signature cheese bread before moving on to hefty portions of soup, salad and the house special: prime rib.

Several leather-bound menus from the Trails Restaurant were retrieved from the trash bin during the restaurant's demolition and are now on display at the Route 66 museums in Victorville and Barstow, as well as the Duarte Historical Museum.

The Trails Restaurant (1952–2001) was a favorite of both locals and out-of-towners. Famous for the lounge entertainment and hefty portions of salad, soup, cheese bread and prime rib, patrons mourned this Route 66 icon's closing. One of the smaller Trails signs is now on display at the Route 66 museum in Victorville, along with the wagon wheel chandelier and Tiffany lamp.

The waitresses were efficient, albeit often cranky. Once, my husband asked the waitress for water, and she replied, "Water? You're lucky you have a chair."

In contrast, auction day presented an alien scene of stacked dishes and glasses, trays and utensils doomed to be hauled off by the highest bidder. Restaurant owners eyed the appliances, while others milled through the rooms, fingering well-used plates and tureens. Artwork that varied from creations by local artists to wood-framed prints purchased decades ago were auctioned off for a buck or two.

As Sylvia Price watched the auction proceed, she seemed puzzled by how she had reached the end of the Trails. It was more than fifty years ago that she and her then-husband, Don, left Kansas in their 1942 Ford coupe and headed for California via Route 66. At age twenty-three, she found work as a waitress at the Willows in Covina and then the Zanzibar Restaurant in Duarte, which today is the Ranchero Mexican Restaurant. Soon after, she landed a job at the Trails, not a bad drive from Covina, where she still resides.

Price recalls serving such stars as Bob Hope and chatting with jockeys from the track, who were regular customers. During the 1970s, the organist was Brook Brown, whose music attracted a large following. She recalled the years when John Owens was the Trails' chef and the sad years when he became ill and she cared for him and his wife. Those were the days when the staff watched out for each other.

Today, Price finds herself unemployed. After thirty-seven years of service, the seventy-two-year-old waitress says she was dressing for her shift when a co-worker called to tell her the restaurant had closed its doors.

Route 66 buffs Dana Rea and John Deeter traveled from Burbank to join in the auction. Both had patronized the Trails for nearly twenty years and "just wanted something of the place to take home." "I'm sorry to see it go," says Dana, who anteed up forty dollars for a painting of a horse and rider that had hung in the main dining room. "The Trails is a piece of Americana along Route 66, and I'll miss it," she said, mourning the loss of a "1960s throwback to the days of Marlboros and bourbon."

While the auctioneer chanted, I watched the excited crowd, as a mounted marlin, caught by the owner off San Clemente in 1963, was sold for $150. To me, that gawking fish was a symbol of happier days, when the future looked bright and exciting and the Trails counted itself among the finer dining establishments in the San Gabriel Valley.

As bidders carried off their prizes, I knew that though they could empty the building of its furnishings, ghosts of days gone by would remain, and echoes of music, singing and laughter would remain until the inevitable day that the building is demolished, leaving one more gaping hole in the legacy of Route 66.

Note: The building was razed in 2002 and replaced with a housing development. Streets at the site have been named in honor of the rooms at the Trails such as Waterfall, Crossroads and Hideaway.

As a teen attending Duarte High School, Jason Golding, Duarte senior planner, worked at the Trails and was instrumental in naming the streets at the Trails' site. "It is our way of honoring the Trails. We were all sad to see it go," Golding lamented. The developer, the City of Duarte and the Duarte Historical Society have placed a plaque on the premises that reads:

The Trails Restaurant started small but vigorous in 1952 on riverbank land acquired in unincorporated territory along a two-lane road known as Highway 66. A welcome stop for travelers, the steak house earned a reputation for its hefty portions, thick soups, crusty cheese bread, and lounge entertainment. When travelers abandoned Route 66 for the new faster freeways, the Trails relied on loyal local patrons.

THE BLVD. CAFE: GONE BUT NOT FORGOTTEN

March 11, 1998

It's our kind of town when a Route 66 icon has vanished but remains in our hearts. Starbucks now occupies the space that was once the most popular burger stand and gathering place in Duarte, the Blvd. Cafe. Arriving in Duarte from Connecticut in 1946, Shirley Halburian was only eight years old, but her memories of the days when her parents, Susie and Tommy Tomasian, owned and operated the café remain vivid.

The Blvd. Cafe was open every day until 2:00 a.m. Shirley would spend her time working, chatting or doing homework with the help of friendly customers, occasionally skipping out across the street with her brother Richard to catch a flick at the Big Sky Drive In.

The land was purchased by the Duarte Redevelopment Agency, and in 1989, the Blvd. Cafe flipped its last burger and poured its last beer. More than one hundred customers came by to say goodbye.

The structure was razed to make way for a shopping center that today is home to Ralphs, Starbucks and other businesses.

Shirley experienced Route 66 throughout its evolution, married George Halburian and raised her family here. She still has her memories and covets a souvenir—the original grill of the Blvd. Cafe. While we've seen the demise of the Big Sky and the Blvd. Cafe, these vanished landmarks remain visible

The Blvd. Cafe flipped its last burger and poured its last beer in 1989, ending a colorful history of dedicated patrons, including stars en route to Hollywood. *Courtesy of the Tomasian family.*

in photos and in publications depicting the history of the San Gabriel Valley and Route 66.

Note: The large Blvd. Cafe sign is on display at the California Route 66 Museum in Barstow. The owners of the café opted for the abbreviated name "Blvd." rather than "Boulevard" because the longer name would have made the sign too big.

Route 66's Blvd. Cafe Comes Back to Life for Fundraiser

August 26, 1998

Ron Pashby of Duarte High School class of 1969 polished up his 1955 Chevy Belair and with his companion, Terri Hager, returned to his hometown to enjoy the bands and to dance at "Friday Nite at the Blvd. Cafe," a tribute to the famed eatery that was founded in 1946 and torn down in 1989. The crowd found itself in the midst of the 1950s while dancing to the sounds of Snotty Scottie & the Hankies and feasting on burgers, potato salad and chili based on the original recipes. The event was held at the Duarte Senior Center and attended by more than three hundred guests. "It's kind of neat," says Mayor Margaret Finlay. "We've got a lot of old and new coming together as the older people introduce a legacy to the younger people."

WHAT DOES THE FUTURE HOLD FOR THE OLD DUARTE SCHOOLHOUSE?

1990

The fate of the 1909 Duarte Schoolhouse at the corner of Buena Vista Street and Central Avenue was being batted about, with preservationists and many Duarte residents calling for the city to save it from demolition. The year? 1987. Now three years later, this reminder of old Rancho de

The 1909 Duarte Schoolhouse was on the brink of becoming a car dealership when, to the delight of all concerned, it was purchased by the Old Spaghetti Factory. Today, it is a favorite haunt of both locals and visitors.

Duarte sits like a punished child, surrounded by barbed wire, dirt and an RV lot.

Note: The building in question was the third Duarte schoolhouse, and thankfully, it was eventually saved from demolition. It now houses the Old Spaghetti Factory, a popular Duarte eatery, and the building has been renovated to its former glory.

THE BRIDGES OF DUARTE

August 22, 2004

Mr. Bradbury's Bridge

The Oak Street Bridge, built in 1908, spans more than an easement and bike trail. The ninety-foot-long bridge links Duarte with its colorful history; joins the community with its neighbor, Bradbury; and creates an excuse to celebrate in unity at our own bridge party. On the evening of September 8, Duarteans will gather beneath the Oak Street Bridge to celebrate its renovation. One of several unique bridges in and near Duarte, one must ask where it got its name, since it spans the present bike trail near the corner of Royal Oaks and Oak Avenue, not Oak Street.

The bridge was often referred to as "Mr. Bradbury's Bridge." The single-span reinforced concrete bridge was erected nearly one hundred years ago to allow for a track-free entrance to the Bradbury estate, home of mining millionaire Lewis Leonard Bradbury.

The story goes that when plans for the Pacific Electric Line were taking shape, permission was needed for a right-of-way through Bradbury's property that would dissect the path leading from town to the estate. It is said that Mr. Bradbury gave his permission on the condition that a bridge would be constructed so that his horse-drawn carriages need not cross over the train tracks. Later automobiles utilized the bridge until 1930, when only pedestrian traffic was allowed across.

Nearly a century after it was built, a grant made the recent renovation possible. Its completion marks the last of a series of projects aimed at improving the trail, which has replaced the tracks on the Pacific Electric right-of-way.

Affectionately known as "Mr. Bradbury's Bridge," this link was born when the Pacific Electric requested a right-of-way through the property of mining millionaire Lewis Leonard Bradbury. He agreed, with the stipulation that a bridge be provided so his carriages need not cross over the tracks.

It was with great foresight that Duarte and Bradbury city officials purchased the abandoned easement in the 1970s, receiving state funds to help develop a pathway for bikers, walkers and equestrians. Few San Gabriel cities followed suit.

Puente Largo Bridge

In 1907, one year before Mr. Bradbury's Bridge was erected, the Puente Largo Railway Bridge was built across the San Gabriel River. Constructed to withstand the weight of freight and passenger trains, it suffered partial collapse during the Great Flood of 1938 when several days of heavy rain inundated the San Gabriel Mountains, causing the dam keepers to open the spillways to release walls of water that threatened to breach the newly built dams. The bridge was immediately renovated with steel spans to allow train traffic to continue.

When the Red Cars ceased running, the bridge was abandoned and once again fell into disrepair. In the late 1980s, the City of Duarte applied for and

The 1907 Puente Largo Bridge spans the San Gabriel River. It was constructed to allow passage of the Pacific Electric to points east. Partially undermined in the Great Flood of 1938, the bridge was quickly rebuilt with steel spans. Today, it is a popular river crossing point for bicyclists, walkers and equestrians.

received a grant to renovate the Puente Largo Bridge. The bridge now links Duarte to the bike path on the east side of the river, allowing access to Azusa Canyon to the north and the ocean to the south, traversing near the 605 Freeway.

Located just a few hundred yards south of Encanto Park, the bridge and bike path have become a major source of recreation for bicyclers, walkers and equestrians throughout the San Gabriel Valley.

PAINTING'S STORY HAS HAPPY ENDING

January 25, 2004

Rosemary La Planche led a colorful life. She was crowned Miss America in 1941 after serving as Miss California for the two previous years. Starring in dozens of films from *Strangler of the Swamp* (1946) to *Golden Hands of Kurigal* (1966), the colorful actress died in May 1979.

Through a strange series of events, La Planche has become a part of Duarte's history.

In the spring of 2003, a painting caught the eye of Kim Anderson of Monrovia as he strolled by Patty's Antiques on South Myrtle Avenue. He was thrilled to see a huge painting of the old Duarte West Santa Fe Depot, which was located near Buena Vista Street and Duarte Road until it was demolished in 1942.

The first depot, named the Butler or East Duarte Depot, was constructed in 1887. Then, years later, that two-story structure was abandoned and later purchased by Dr. Norman Morrison, Santa Fe chief surgeon, and moved to his ranch, which we know today as Westminster Gardens. It has since been razed. A second depot, known as the West Duarte Depot, was built in 1897 on the northeast corner of Buena Vista Street and Duarte Road. It was retired in 1941 and demolished the next year. The stationmaster's house, located across the street, remains today.

Anderson declared that the painting belonged to the Duarte Historical Museum to be on display for everyone to enjoy. But as luck would have it, before the museum was able to purchase this prize, it was sold.

Clarke Moseley, former city attorney for Duarte and current city attorney for El Monte, had finished lunching with friends on Myrtle Avenue one day when a painting in Patty's Antiques caught his eye. On careful examination, he declared it a "must have," and "after intense negotiations," he was the proud owner of the painting of the Duarte West Santa Fe Depot.

From the start, Moseley intended to exhibit the painting in his home to enjoy for a few months and then donate it to the Duarte Historical Museum. He recently made a gift of the painting to the museum, where it is proudly displayed.

This story could end here, but there is more to the saga! Geraldine England, now an Azusa resident, came to Duarte in 1952, graduating from Duarte High School in 1965. Her best friends, Raymond and Barbara Lindsay, owned a business called Western Select, located on Hamilton Road near the railroad tracks.

One day, Barbara commissioned an artist to create a painting of the Duarte West Santa Fe Depot from a photograph she had acquired from some historical archives. The painting would be a gift to her husband for display in their offices. Raymond and Barbara already owned several paintings by the artist Rosemary La Planche, who had retired from show business and was enjoying a quieter life as an artist. La Planche died a few years after painting the depot.

When Western Select closed, the owners gave the painting to Geraldine, who had coveted it for nearly twenty years. Her son Troy, thirty-seven, graduated from Duarte High School in 1985. "The painting was always there, an integral part of our home," he said. He was saddened when lack of space resulted in his mother's announcement that she was selling the treasure through Patty's Antique Store and hoped it would find an owner who would appreciate its historical value.

The Englands are thrilled that the chain of events set in motion so many years ago ended with the painting by this flamboyant actress being displayed at the museum.

THE OLD DUARTE MARKET: HISTORIC BUILDING FINDS NEW FACE

March 21, 2004

It was once the focal point of town, the place where residents gathered, swapped stories, picked up mail and stocked up on groceries. It was built before the turn of the century.

Left up to Collette Aragon, it will once more be a safe haven for adults and children to leave behind the stresses of life; a place to socialize and maybe even learn to dance in the process. The Old Duarte Market at the southwest corner of Highland and Royal Oaks has changed faces many times, but one could never guess what was coming next.

Following the years it served as a central meeting place for rural Duarte, it was purchased in the 1970s as an investment by Collette and Nestor Aragon. Thereafter, it was rented by the Aragons to a multitude of enterprises, including a meat and produce market, a boutique and beauty shop, a flower shop and a karate studio, to name a few.

In 1994, it was opened by the owners as Nestor's Carpets, but Collette had some ideas of her own—a dream she was about to make sure would come true. Two passions drove the English-born Collette. She yearned to renovate the building to its original luster and reopen it as a dance studio.

With perseverance and hard work, both of her visions have materialized. After stripping the floor of several layers of covering, Collette and Nestor

Built before the turn of the century, the Old Duarte Market has changed faces many times throughout the years. Once the popular meeting place where residents could pick up mail and groceries, run into old friends and perhaps use the phone, it has housed a score of entities since then, including a carpet store, karate school, beauty parlor, dance studio, gadget store and dog wash. *Courtesy of the Duarte Historical Museum.*

exposed the building's original floor, which they say dates back to 1879. "It was in terrible shape and has sustained major water damage," Collette said. They cleaned, re-stained and varnished the Douglas-fir floor until it was smooth and shiny enough for the feet of dancers. With things looking up, they likewise ripped out the fake ceiling, discovering the original wood ceiling and skylight.

The original building was two stories, and Collette believes the basement was originally the first floor. During renovation work, they discovered some signs of the past, including an old chute that they believe was used when the building housed the post office.

Eventually, Nestor moved his carpets to the back, and Collette's dance studio was born.

Note: Eventually, this too came to an end, and after a series of enterprises housed in the historical building, it is now home to two entities—one a gadget store and the other the EZ Dog Wash, owned by Duarte sisters Linda Alashti and Aida Otero.

WHAT'S IN A STREET NAME? A CITY'S HISTORY

January 14, 2001

Few people in Monrovia and Duarte have heard of Banana Street or Falling Leaf Avenue. When streets were extended from Los Angeles to the east during 1918 and 1929, many local avenues lost their original names—names that are all but forgotten by now.

Fortunately, our local historian, Steve Baker, has researched the subject and can readily recite street names that can't be found on any modern map.

Many of Monrovia's streets are named after fruits and plants, such as Lemon, Lime, Orange, Palm and Ivy. Other streets honored presidents—McKinley, Lincoln and Madison. In the same vein, Hillcrest Avenue was originally dubbed Banana Street because of the many banana trees that lined its path.

White Oak was the original name of Foothill, and Huntington Drive, known for many years as Route 66, was originally named Falling Leaf Avenue. Royal Oaks Avenue was once known as Duarte Avenue, but the name was changed to distinguish it from Duarte Road. Las Lomas Avenue, once a small access road, was named Whiting Avenue, while Bradbourne was known as Georgi, named so for a garage that was once located there.

Duarte Road experienced many name changes, from County Road to Main Street to Santa Fe.

Driving around Duarte's Fish Canyon area today, I am amused to see how many streets appear as one word on one street sign and two words on another, such as Opal Canyon/Opalcanyon and Mountaincrest/Mountain Crest.

I always assumed a discovery of opals in the area was responsible for the naming of Opal Canyon, but Baker reports that Melcanyon and Opalcanyon were named after Mel and Opal Wiley, who once lived in the canyon.

Duarte's most famous street sign is probably that of Cinco Robles, after which a popular song was written in the 1950s by Larry Sullivan.

Several years ago, there was a move in Duarte to change the name of Betty Hill Drive to Glenn Miller Drive, in honor of the home built on that street by the famous bandleader. That home was destroyed in the 1980 fire, and the name-change movement fizzled.

MAPPING THE RANCHOS

May 2010

Thanks to the efforts of curator Irwin Margiloff, two historic maps are now on display at the Duarte Historical Museum for the benefit of the public. These maps—one dated 1858 and located in the National Archives and the other detailing the first subdivision of the Duarte Rancho—have been reproduced and unveiled with little fanfare.

When California entered the Union, a land commission was formed to examine the validity of the roughly nine hundred Spanish and Mexican land grants. When Andres Duarte's claim was found to be valid, the commission required that a map be prepared. Lawyer-surveyor Henry

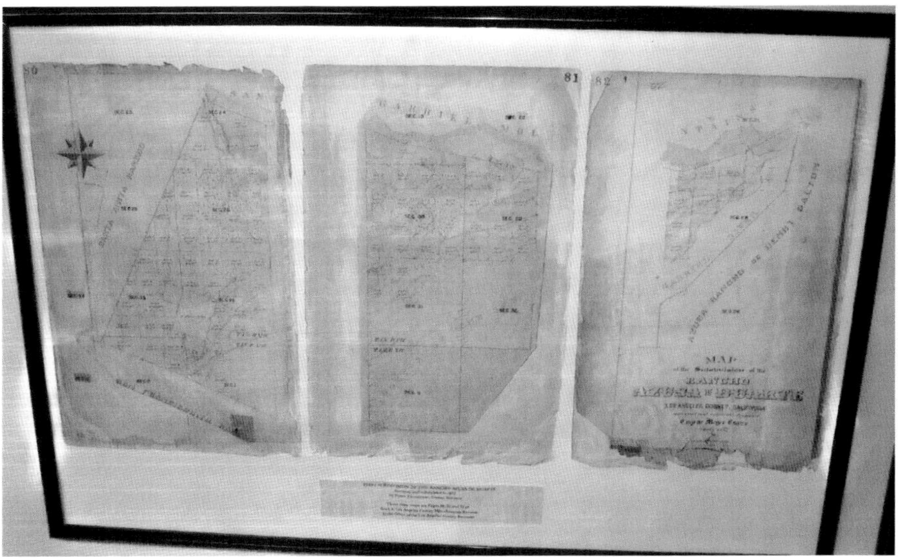

Thanks to the efforts of curator Irwin Margiloff, these maps are on display at the Duarte Historical Museum.

Hancock prepared the first survey of the Duarte Rancho with true surveying instruments.

Hancock's map shows that the Duarte Rancho sits on top of the San Bernardino Base Line, a very important reference line for real estate in Southern California. Various clerical notations show that although the land grant was held valid in 1858, protracted legal issues were raised, and Duarte's rancho was not "patented" to him until 1878, by which time he and many other original land grant claimants had died.

Curator Margiloff scanned the map and recently printed it in full color. A black-and-white version is in the Duarte edition of *Images of America*, which was released last year. The 1858 map is displayed in the museum's Citrus Room.

A framed copy of the first subdivision map of the Duarte Rancho is exhibited next to the Hancock map. Drawn in 1872 by Frank Lecouvreur, the county surveyor, it was mounted on three pages of Book 6 of the county's *Miscellaneous Records*. The map notes that it was created at the request of Eugene Meyer and illustrates watercourses and irrigation ditches, native shelters ("jackalls"), topographic features and a few buildings, in addition to the ownership of many of the parcels, most of which were forty acres in size.

The three-part map is referred to in almost all transfers of land in Duarte. It is in poor physical condition, probably from repeated copying. In fact, the pages had fallen out of Book 6's binding several years ago. "We were given permission by the manager of public documents to set up a scanning operation in the dungeon-like basement records room of the recorder's office in Norwalk and scanned it in full color," says Margiloff. It too was recently printed and framed and is an attractive companion to Hancock's map.

Monrovia Days of Flying

September 2010

The Monrovia Airport, Alias Foothill Flying Field, 1928 to 1953 chronicles a piece of local history that is probably remembered by only a few of our senior residents. The book reflects a man's love and respect for his two pilot brothers and records historical events that might otherwise be lost.

"In the beginning, there was the Rancho Azusa de Duarte, which covered all of our local areas and then some," writes author John R. Irwin. "The Bradbury Estates, Inc. apparently owned the parts of the Ranch that would eventually become the Monrovia Airport."

Monrovia Airport? That is news to many local residents. In the 1920s and '30s, many San Gabriel cities such as Pasadena, Monrovia and Altadena had their own airports or landing strips. The local one, referred to as "the friendliest little airport in the country," was established in about 1928 through the Monrovia Air Club organized by Don Robertson and with the help of the Union Oil Company of Los Angeles. It was eventually approved for commercial operations. The author's two older brothers, Kal and Louis, were pilots deeply involved in the airport and its activities.

The younger Irwin poignantly describes his youthful infatuation with the field. "In 1932, when I was nine years old, I spent many very special Sunday afternoons with my family parked along the north side of a long vacant lot about a block south of Huntington Drive just east of Shamrock Street, in the city of Monrovia," he writes. "People came from miles around to watch the fabric-covered airplanes rumble down the dirt runway, take off, perform stunts and land again. The spectators used their cars as makeshift bleachers."

As an adult, Irwin was disappointed when he read a history book about Monrovia and the airport was not mentioned. He decided to memorialize all that he could learn about the subject and began by interviewing his brother Kal's widow. She was able to fill him in on many of the facts and provide him with photos and other memorabilia, which he reproduced in the book. She also gave him contact information for others who were involved in the airport during its days of glory.

This small airport was the scene of many activities such as flying lessons, airplane repair and storage, fire lookout flights, flying hearse services, charter trips, sign towing and mail flights. Air shows were also popular events. Everyone liked to watch a jumper parachute from two thousand feet. The airport's star jumper, Ralph Wiggins, made the first jump of his life during an air show when the scheduled jumper had failed show up. He made his last one in 1999 on his seventy-ninth birthday.

The airport has been a movie location favorite since 1915. *The Great Plane Robbery* was filmed there, as was *The Fighting Pilot*. Probably the most notable movie filmed at the Monrovia Airport was *20,000 Men a Year*, starring Randolph Scott and Preston Foster.

MENUS GIVE TASTE OF LIFE IN DECADES

August 2007

Peruse an old restaurant menu and a nostalgic cord will most probably twang, evoking memories of those eateries so reminiscent of days gone by—and also those modest prices! Remember the quarter-pounder hamburger meal for the price of forty cents? That was the typical cost in the 1950s at such restaurant chains as the Snack Shop in Orange County.

Menus old and new are on display at the Duarte Historical Museum from the collection of Mark Montgomery. Born and raised in Duarte, Montgomery graduated from Duarte High School in 1988. His passion for frequenting garage sales, antique stores and museums has rendered him a collector. In addition to menus, Montgomery has extensive collections of license plates, car brochures, cookbooks, owners' manuals for now-obsolete kitchen appliances and Hot Wheels.

In 1943, Twohey's Family Restaurant opened on Arroyo Boulevard in Pasadena. With seating for thirty-seven customers, the establishment soon adopted a clothespin and tears logo entitled "Home of the Little Stink-O," adopted when a woman was aghast at a gentleman seated next to her who was generously garnishing his hamburger with onions and pickles. "O Stinko!" she purportedly blurted out. A Twohey's remains today in Alhambra.

A late 1940s menu from the Carolina Pines on Melrose in Hollywood, opened in 1923, reads, "May we suggest a martini or Manhattan with your meal?" Montgomery's oldest menu, although undated, is from the original Pioneer Tamale Restaurant, touting "Purveyors of fine food since 1888." It was located in Stockton, the "gateway to the fabulous mother lode country."

A 1952 menu from one of the famous Stans proclaims, "Our car attendants will be happy to have your baby's bottle or baby food promptly warmed," while a 1950 menu from Dolores' proudly states, "Adventures in Good Eating: Recommended by Duncan Hines." Other menus are from El Cholo; a 1949 menu from Wimpys; and one from Yellow Basket, a small chain of restaurants in Santa Ana, Menifee and Temecula.

A modern menu from a restaurant that Montgomery finds unique comes from Annias Kitchen, located at the El Monte Airport. He enjoys watching the planes take off and land while eating, especially on Tuesday evenings, when the eatery features ham hocks and lima beans.

Also on the unique side, the collection features a menu from the Horseless Carriage, which is located in the North Hills Galpin Ford Dealership. "It is unique to have a full restaurant within a car dealership," says Montgomery. The Horseless Carriage menu includes the Galpinburger and boasts 100 percent pure buffalo in its buffalo chili.

An obviously dated menu is from Knotts Berry Farm, where chicken dinners are still famous today. Starting out in the 1920s selling berries and then full pies, the original Knotts Berry Farm restaurant served its first dinner in 1934 to twenty customers. By popular demand, it was serving three hundred dinners by 1937 and continued to flourish through the years as one of Southern California's must-visit spots for tourists and locals alike.

DUARTE CHAMBER OF COMMERCE BROCHURE OF 1941

November 2006

In a brochure created by the Duarte Chamber of Commerce, many attributes of the community were praised, not the least of which was "hospitality." The brochure claims:

> *Following the tradition established by Don Andres Duarte, the community has been famous for its hospitality from early pioneer days. The beautiful homes...in fragrant orange groves...have been the destination of friends from the lower valley and cities. Duarte folks are glad to welcome friend or stranger into their home circle.*

Printed in 1941 to commemorate the "One Hundredth Anniversary of the Andres Duarte Land Grant and the Community that Bears His Name," the brochure recites historical facts including the local discovery of gold, local landmarks and "social clubs." It goes on to state, "In the early fifties, Felipe Duarte's wife discovered a large pocket of gold in a small canyon back of the 'Homestead' and quite a gold rush was started." The Homestead refers to the adobe home built by Andres Duarte, the site of which is located on Tocino Drive. According to the brochure, "Several mines were opened in the hills, and many prospected the San Gabriel Canyon with varied success. Between 1852 and 1896, it was estimated that over 'two million' in gold was taken from this district."

While today Duarte's coveted "landmarks" consist of Route 66 icons long since gone, the 1941 brochure claims celebrity in several homes: "One of the oldest landmarks in the community is the Mrs. Nellie Morin home on Duarte Road," purchased by her father, Allan Sandefur, in 1875. "Before that time, the house was the tavern at which the stage coach passengers stopped for the first night on their trip from San Pedro to inland towns on the Camino Real San Gabriel–San Bernardino, now Duarte Road."

Among the civic organizations touted in the brochure are the Duarte Reading Circle (founded in 1909 and viable, though waning, today), Girl Scouts, Campfire Girls, 4-H Club ("agricultural for boys and home making for girls") and "The Friendly Indians."

One startling alleged fact described in the brochure details the fate of the family of the only son of Andres Duarte. While in Mexico, forty-year-old Felipe was killed by Indians. His widow remarried and bore five children, one of whom, Mrs. Maria de Jesus Lope-Duarte-Maron, who lived on Mountain Avenue, died at the age of 100. According to the brochure, her mother outlived her, dying in 1935 at the age of 141!

Route 66 Parades: A Duarte Tradition

Many in Duarte had talked about the idea of an annual parade, but none spoke too loudly. In this town, if you announce an idea, you are immediately put in charge of it, and no one wanted to commit to organizing something as grand as a parade. Then Tim Lowry came to town and not only talked about a parade but also offered to head up a committee. The year was 1996. The Duarte Community Coordinating Council was where he expressed this desire, and there was a lot of excitement and offers of help. Almost immediately it was decided to work around the theme "Salute to Route 66," and the first parade committee was formed. As the parade was being planned, pre-parade activities and fundraisers started to pop up. An all-day car caravan drove along Route 66, stopping at many of the icons along the way to the Route 66 Museums in Victorville and Barstow. The Duarte Historical Museum created a Route 66 exhibit. The grand marshal of this first annual parade was none other than Bobby Troup, who rode in a 1948 Buick convertible.

The next year, another successful parade was held, featuring a commemorative parade pin depicting the Big Sky Drive In. The Duarte Historical Museum sponsored a bus trip along Route 66 to the Bagdad Café in Newberry Springs, and a sock hop was held to raise money for the

Duarte's first annual Salute to Route 66 Parade in 1996. The grand marshal was none other than Bobby Troup, who rode in a 1948 Buick convertible. It was a grand success, paving the way for the future parades.

parade committee. The grand marshal that year was KTLA newsman Stan Chambers, along with five Los Angeles TV children's show icons: "Sheriff John" Rovick, "Engineer Bill" Stulla, "Skipper Frank" Herman, Mary Ann King of *Romper Room* and *Popeye* host Tom Hatten.

And so, year after year, new parade committees were formed, organizing meetings were held year-round to plan the upcoming parade and a tradition flourished. In September 2012, the seventeenth annual Salute to Route 66 Parade was held.

FIESTA DAY PARADE OF THE '60S

September 9, 2012

As the anticipation mounted, cars lined Huntington Drive, and the procession began. Flags, horses, bands, floats, cars and even army tanks proudly entertained the excited crowds. But wait! Where is the sidewalk?

Where is the median? We were watching a Super 8 film transferred to VHS and later to DVD of the Duarte 1960 Fiesta Day Parade, originally shot by Joe Murphy.

Approaching the seventeenth annual Salute to Route 66 Parade, we are reminded that in days gone by, Duarteans have often enjoyed parades,

"Get Fit on Route 66" was the theme of the seventeenth annual Salute to Route 66 Parade in September 2012. Featuring both new and retro cars, high school bands, equestrians and local celebrities, scores of volunteers made it happen.

picnics and fiestas along our little stretch of Route 66 and in local parks and private venues.

Cars that lined the 1960 parade mirror the ones that appear in today's event, only now they are referred to as "retro" or "vintage." Back then, they were new! The scene through Duarte in the 1960s is noticeably different, with scattered businesses, empty lots and no median as we have today.

Rafael Castillas, Duarte's public works manager, says that the Huntington Drive median island improvements occurred through a series of projects. The city constructed and installed a majority of the median islands, landscaping and street-name monument signs in 1975. In the 1990s, street-name monuments were replaced with the Mission Bells. In 1991, the bus shelters and furniture were constructed and installed along the Huntington corridor.

A Fiesta de Duarte was held for years during the 1940s and '50s. Similar to our current city picnic, it featured exhibits and food booths, concerts, square dancing and even a lively tug-o-war. The event lasted for several days and was held at a private facility called Swiss Park, which sadly is no longer here.

Primitive Huntington Drive was flanked by orange groves interrupted by small businesses such as Honeyville, where the fragrance of fresh-squeezed citrus permeated the air and jars of honey attracted passersby. At the corner of Huntington Drive and Bradbourne, a cluster of businesses existed, including Randell's Gas Station and Fruit Stand and Fishman's Fruit Stand. Highland and Huntington was another spot where businesses formed. Old-timers recall fondly the Old Kentucky Home and Brown's Restaurants. The first traffic light was installed at the corner of Huntington and Las Lomas in 1957.

And why is there a parade? It started out and remains to be the result of grass-roots groups—Duarteans with volunteerism in their hearts. The parade committee shoulders numerous responsibilities with the organizing,

Duarte old-timers fondly remember Honeyville. Besides honey, patrons thirsted after the freshly squeezed orange juice that was so popular when citrus ranches dotted the town. *Courtesy of the Duarte Historical Museum.*

planning and logistics of the parade. Of course, the city helps, and the businesses chip in. But it's really the volunteers who give so freely of their time and energy who make it happen. Cheers to the parade committee!

Salute to Route 66—A Parade with a Surprise

October 1, 2006

Imagine my surprise on Saturday morning at 7:00 a.m. while driving on Huntington Drive to the parade VIP breakfast when, suddenly, a vision before me came into focus through the blinding sun. It was our beautiful bronzed statue in all its glory strapped onto a flatbed truck. As it glistened in the morning light, I watched our city's namesake, Don Andres Duarte, straddling his stallion and traveling through what was once his rancho. I wondered what he would think of our town today in contrast to the wild, dusty lands he was once commissioned to protect.

What a sight to behold! The bronze statue of Andres Avelino Duarte on his stallion gave parade viewers a preview of the wondrous creation that was to be unveiled in an upcoming ceremony. Once again, the proud mayordomo and his stallion rode through the rancho he so loved.

Later in the morning, when the parade procession began, I watched the spectators as they lined Duarte's Route 66. To the last one they were smiling, yelling, laughing and waving. Community pride was at its height—from the gigantic American flag toted by members of the Church of Jesus Christ of Latter Day Saints to the screaming fire engine that marked the parade's finale. And the biggest surprise of the day was the statue, which followed the Duarte in Bronze banner and Andres Duarte look-alike, Leandro Orozco, on his horse flanked by costumed children from Los 3 Amigos.

The parade committee, composed of citizen volunteers and led by President K.C. Caracci, must be commended for an excellent job. And the selection of Dr. Michael Friedman, president and chief executive officer of the City of Hope, was a fitting choice for the grand marshal. He was gracious indeed and greeted warmly by all. As the last of the parade passed by, the crowds headed for Royal Oaks Park for the traditional city picnic.

Salute to Route 66—Our Kind of Parade

October 2012

It was Duarte's day to shine, and under a picture-perfect sky, Huntington Drive, our little stretch of Route 66, was alive with activity in anticipation of the seventeenth annual Salute to Route 66 Parade. Mr. Y and his Duarte High School students set up cameras and sound equipment, sheriff cars patrolled the area and, as early as 8:00 a.m., spectators were placing chairs and umbrellas under trees, anticipating hot weather.

Meanwhile at the Duarte Community Center, members of the Duarte Woman's Club, sporting their club aprons, set tables to prepare for the crowds. Breakfast was prepared by Chef Louis Rice and his Duarte High School ROP culinary arts students. There the city council and parade participants received last-minute instructions, and introductions were made. Outside, cars slipped into their assigned spots at the various staging areas. Bands practiced, cheerleaders cheered, dancers danced, horses became impatient and children tried to stay calm.

As the procession began, it appeared perfectly organized. Little did the public know the chaos behind the scenes. The parade committee is composed of volunteers, with the help of city staff, local businesses and community organizations. This year, obstacles were many, and they occurred at a crucial time. Parade organizer Lisa Magno became ill and had to drop out, but true to form in our town, replacements jumped in to help. Former parade chair K.C. Caracci filled in as co-chair together with former mayor Lois Gaston.

There were many vintage cars on display at the post-parade picnic, thanks to the efforts of Richard Campbell.

Also stepping in to be sure things went smoothly was Buffy Aikens, who coordinated the lineup, signs and cars, while Lupe Valerio coordinated the help of city employees. The bands were organized by Tony Molina. "It was a Herculean effort by Ermias Bitow, who coordinated the tables, chairs and sound systems, including delivery, set up and retrieval," says Caracci. "There were many more volunteers eager to see a successful parade—too many to list, but our thanks go to them all."

The Mystery Song of Duarte

2005

There is a mystery surrounding a song entitled "Ode to Duarte"; no one seems to know details about the songwriter or when it was written.

"Ode to Duarte"
Written by Rosamond Norman)
(To the tune of "Isle of Capri")

Duarte of thee we sing, dear old Duarte
Beloved of thy beauties so wondrously fair
Foothills and mountains above us so stately
Orange blossoms perfuming the air
Mockingbirds sing in the moonlight
Filling all the nights with song
Blue jays flying 'mong the orange trees
Scold and chatter all day long
And there is no place more fair, more lovely
Where all the people are friendly and kind
Look o'er our country from ocean to ocean
No place better than Duarte you'll find.

Chapter 2

PEOPLE

Who are the people of Duarte? Of course, there are the "plain folk" who landed in town for various reasons, many hoping to improve their health with the warm, dry weather. There were colorful historical figures, pioneers who landed here by design or default and built the first schools, established ranches and created the building blocks of our community—to name a few: Captain Gerald P. Fitzgerald of Her Majesty's Irish Guard; the Reverend David S. Shrode, who established Duarte's first Sunday school; and John Scott, the first horticulture commissioner of Los Angeles County. Other well-known personalities followed, like the big-band leader Glenn Miller, the 1979 Pulitzer Prize–winning playwright Sam Shepard and prolific author Roderick Thorpe. Before the arrival of all these people, the Gabrielino Indians inhabited the area, living peacefully in the foothills and enjoying the gifts of the lovely San Gabriel River.

The Grand Lady of Duarte

April 6, 2003

Today, she lives a quiet life in Duarte, spending time at the Senior Center and enjoying friends and neighbors. One would never guess she is the Grand Lady of Duarte, our town's last local living link to the man for whom our

Victoria Duarte Cordova (May 19, 1912–January 20, 2005) was the great-great-granddaughter of Andres Avelino Duarte, born on the family ranch in Duarte located on the site of the present-day Maxwell School.

city was named. Victoria Duarte Cordova is the great-great-granddaughter of Andres Duarte.

What fascinates me most about this lady is not her long Duarte ancestral line but the fact that she was born in this town in 1912 on a ranch once located across from where Maxwell School sits today. "In which hospital were you born?" I naively asked her in a recent interview. "Hospital?" she laughed. "Everyone had their babies at home back then." Her insistence on making her debut occurred on a May day as her mother watched the Monrovia Day Parade. A short time later, Vicki was born on the eleven-acre ranch of her great-great-grandparents.

Vicki recalls her younger days with fondness: "We had a well and pumped our water, and when the horse trough was full, it was considered a fun job to walk the horse from the stable to the water. Secretly, I was afraid of the horse, fearful it would step on my feet."

The pit toilets, wood stove, citrus trees and farm animals add to her memories. And most of all she loved the family dinners—particularly on special occasions when tamales were served.

Vicki remembers that Mountain Avenue was then unpaved. She and her mother would catch a "jitney" to Myrtle Avenue in Monrovia, where they could visit the post office, shop or hop onto a streetcar for longer trips. When her parents separated, she and her mother lived in Pacoima, then San Gabriel, then Arcadia, but still Vicki called Duarte home, visiting often the ranch that was handed down through the family until it was sold in 1940.

She married a man of Mexican descent, a driver for Corpe Bros. Ranches. "Why he picked me, I'll never know," she admitted. "I was wild, loved to go dancing and socialize. He was a wonderful man but closed-mouthed and quiet."

After his death in 1990, Vicki sold their Arcadia home and returned to stay in the town she had always called home. Even today she serves as a docent at our local museum and, until recently, volunteered as a guide at the San Gabriel Mission, where her great-great-grandmother, Eulalia Perez de Guillen, once served as keeper of the keys.

Note: The Grand Lady of Duarte died on January 20, 2005. She is buried at the San Gabriel Mission. Many tributes to her life appeared in local papers, such as the following one written by this author.

Victoria Duarte de Cordova

February 2005

To her friends, she was simply Vicki. Technically, she was Victoria Petronila Gertrudes Sarradell Duarte de Cordova. To the town of Duarte, where

Despite her much-celebrated name, Victoria Petronila Gertrudes Sarradell Duarte de Cordova was a familiar sight around town during the last decade of her life. She served as a docent at the Duarte Historical Museum and liked socializing at the senior center. She always said, "Please just call me Vicki."

she was born, she was the great-great-granddaughter of the city's namesake, Andres Avelino Duarte. To all, she was a grand lady who seemed amused at her celebrity status and accepted it with humility. Vicki died of natural causes on January 20, 2005.

A dedicated member of the Duarte Historical Society, Vicki served at the museum for decades and donated many family heirlooms that remain on display today. She also spent many years serving as a guide at the San Gabriel Mission.

Several months ago, the historical society offered to spearhead a fundraising campaign to erect a bronze statue of Andres Duarte and his horse. The campaign became known as "Duarte in Bronze."

Sculptor Richard Myer studied the life of Andres Duarte and then created two clay statues, one of which would be a prototype for the final work. Some committee members felt the statue depicting Andres Duarte as a soldier was appropriate. He served in the Mexican army until his retirement in 1841, at which time he was granted nearly seven thousand acres that became Rancho Azusa de Duarte.

The second statue reflected Duarte's life as a rancher, sitting on his horse and gazing across the acres of land he had acquired. As a rancher, he raised cattle, horses and sheep and marked them with his brand, the familiar Duarte "D."

When the soldier-versus-rancher issue culminated in an impasse, the committee placed the decision in the hands of the only living local link to the

Sculptor/artist Richard Myer created several clay prototypes leading up to the final statue of Andres Avelino Duarte on his horse. The decision had to be made: soldier or rancher? Victoria Duarte Cordova was saddled with this dilemma and in the end announced her preference to be "rancher!"

Duarte family. Vicki studied the statues, praised the sculptor and decisively announced that the rancher would be the most appropriate.

Living across the street from City Hall, Vicki quietly continued her genealogy research, hoping to trace her family's roots as far back as records would allow. She studied quietly, mostly on her own or with the help of Irwin Margiloff, museum curator, and historian Steve Baker. Since the inception of the Route 66 Parade, Vicki anxiously looked forward to representing the Duarte Museum, riding in the company of family members or with Baker. She was scheduled to ride in the 2004 parade but at the last minute was not physically able to participate. She watched the festivities from the sidelines, receiving handshakes and hugs from passersby.

EVERETT ADAMS: MEMORIES OF THE PAST

May 7, 2009

It was a Duarte that lingers in the memory of only a handful of people—a land of disappearing mountains, German prisoners of war, glowworms and Hopalong Cassidy. At age seventy-six, Everett Adams remembers it all like it was yesterday. Not only was Everett born and raised in Duarte, but his parents were also born here. His grandfather, he says, came to this area seeking work with the famed Lucky Baldwin.

The Duarte that dominates Everett's recollections is alive with the aroma of citrus groves, dusty unpaved streets and wide-open spaces that beckoned him to explore on horseback.

Everett's father, Milton, worked on the Baird Ranch, where he supervised the workers. At the outset, he and his wife, Bertha, shared a small house on the ranch with the gardener, who tended the Baird's Japanese gardens. But

Everett Adams holds a wealth of memories about Duarte's early days. His father, Milton Adams, worked as a supervisor on the Baird citrus ranch, where Everett and his siblings led a carefree life until Milton's tragic death.

Left to right: Howard, Everett, Milton Jr. and Stanley Adams. The children of Milton Adams befriended German prisoners of war who picked oranges on the Baird Ranch, watched a mountain mysteriously disappear and rode their horses along the foothills. *Courtesy of Everett Adams.*

as Milton's family grew (eventually to seven children), the gardener and his wife moved out. Born in 1933, the decades were happy ones for Everett and his siblings, with plenty of space to roam and play.

Everett recalls the looming mountain behind the ranch that he and his siblings would often climb. Then, one day, men in trucks arrived, surveyed the mountain and started hauling it away. The clay dirt was just what was needed for the construction of the Santa Anita Dam, and eventually, the entire mountain was gone and the dam completed. "We could never get used to that big mountain disappearing," says Everett.

Then there was the time during World War II when buses brought German prisoners of war to the ranch. "They were all officers, and though they worked hard, they weren't very good at orange picking," Everett recalls. "We used to hang around and try to talk with them. They were always friendly." He recalls that the buses would take the POWs to the Three Peppers, a local restaurant and bar, so they could drink beer. "The racial climate was such that they wouldn't allow my father in, so he waited outside."

The house that the Duarte Historical Museum now occupies in Encanto Park was moved there from the corner of Cotter and Royal Oaks Drive where the Church of Jesus Christ of Latter Day Saints now stands. It was probably in the 1940s, Everett recalls, that every time the family passed that house, his folks would say, "This is where Hopalong Cassidy lives." Presumably, they were talking about the actor William Boyd, and at present, there is a frenzy of research with an aim to verify that Hopalong Cassidy was, in fact, a Duartean. So far, no concrete information to prove this belief has been found.

Everett, who still lives in Duarte, colorfully describes places and events buried in Duarte's past, such as swimming in the reservoir, hunting for glowworms and eating at the Chapel Inn. He remembers the small airport in Monrovia and watching the parachutists landing there. He fondly recalls helping his father haul oranges on a wagon pulled by their two horses, Kate and Babe. When Babe died, Kate became rather wild, but Everett learned to ride her. Eventually, he became an expert horseman, riding his golden palomino named Goldie. "We learned to ride at the E.B. Green Ranch in Monrovia, where I won trophies, even though we couldn't afford a saddle and had to ride bareback." He also recalls riding in the Monrovia Day parades.

The sad memories haunt him, bringing tears even today. At the age of fifty-five, Everett's father suffered a heart attack while driving his car on Royal Oaks Drive. The car rolled over the embankment and under the Bradbury Bridge. There he died, survived by his wife and seven children. After that, the family moved off the ranch.

Everett is the product of local schools. He attended Huntington and Clifton Schools in Monrovia and then Monrovia-Arcadia-Duarte (MAD) High School, where he was a football star, playing on the varsity team three out of his four years. He remembers those days vividly. "My mom would pile us into her Model A and drive us all to school," he recalls. When he was older, he would take the Red Car to school. After graduating from Pasadena City College, he worked for Avery Label for thirty years.

ALOYSIA MOORE: COAUTHOR OF *ON THE DUARTE*

November 18, 1998

Aloysia Denman Moore was a journalist, author, activist and dedicated volunteer. Her many accomplishments in Duarte from the time she arrived in 1946 were so outstanding that the city named a park after her.

Aloysia was loved and admired, and her recent passing is a great loss to all who knew her. A native Californian and graduate of Fresno State College, she worked as a freelance journalist and designer of children's toys. Arriving in Duarte, she was an activist from day one. She was a founding member of the Duarte Woman's Club, which was organized in 1949, and throughout the years, she was an active member of the Reading Circle and Garden Club. She was also a founding member of the Duarte Historical Society and served as its third president (1967–68). But she is perhaps best remembered as coauthor of *On the Duarte*, the only comprehensive book dedicated to the history of our town.

In a recent interview by Mary Barrow Somerlott that aired on Duarte's Public Access Channel, DCTV, Aloysia recalled her early days in Duarte. During the postwar era, there was a flurry of local construction, with young couples moving in and starting families. During those days, the telephone company was unable to keep up with the overwhelming demand, a worrisome fact to young women, especially those expecting babies. Aloysia was the proud owner of the first telephone on her block, and she had it installed in the garage so that her neighbors could have easy access if they needed to make a call.

When Anna Wallace began writing her book *Devil Grass*, a history of towns in the San Gabriel Valley, she knew where to go for help. Aloysia gave freely of her incredible knowledge about local history. Anna recalls Aloysia fondly: "She was a history buff, but she was also walking history."

Through her mother, Rena Denman—who lived well past one hundred years and passed away only last year—Aloysia was connected to an illustrious Spanish family and was related to the Bannings of Wilmington. She loved to tell stories of playing with the Banning children at the M Street Mansion, which is now a museum. Her eyes would sparkle as she gave her companion a poke with her elbow. "And kid," she would say to a listener who had not been a kid for fifty or more years, "you just ought to have seen…" and off she would go on another animated tale of the past.

Aloysia ran for Duarte City Council in the early 1960s, losing by five votes. In the next election, she ran again, losing by eight votes. Subsequently, she was appointed to the city council to replace a member leaving during his term. After two years of serving, she was elected to the post for another four.

She waged a powerful fight against those who were determined to bring poker parlors to Duarte, and in the end, she prevailed. Her greatest accomplishment was lobbying for a library. The sorry library that was behind where the Bank of America now stands was inadequate and plagued with a leaking roof. Patrons had to dodge the buckets that collected the invasive rain. According to Aloysia, the city council voted down a new library. "Previously, I thought I had to behave like a man to get my way," she said in an interview. "Finally, I decided I would act like a woman!"

She spearheaded a library club, which consisted mostly of wives of the important men in town, and together they fought for the library that serves us today. It was a loss to the community when Aloysia and her husband, Richard, moved away. I remember how she called me after her move and was still chuckling because she had moved to Dallas, Oregon, and her furniture went to Dallas, Texas.

Her husband, who was always at her side, died a few years after the move.

THE LLAMA LADY

February 3, 2011

"Was I seeing things?" I asked myself recently as I spied a most unusual sight on Royal Oaks Drive near Mount Olive. On the roadside, a lady was walking a beautiful llama. This, I thought, is certainly a story worth pursuing.

As it turns out, the lady is not the owner but the llama's sitter, known around town as the "Llama Lady." A resident of Duarte for eighteen years, Eileen Harrington Robinson takes care of animals for their owners, but admittedly that practice has always been with dogs. She is extremely passionate about animals and loves to feed, train, walk and care for them. Sixteen-month-old Copper, affectionately called "KoKo," is her first llama. The owner, a firefighter who lives in Bradbury, trusts Copper's care to Eileen, who started caring for him when he was a baby. At his home, Copper enjoys the company of two adult llamas and his five-month-old sister, Bella.

"Llamas don't like to be touched on the head or approached abruptly," says Eileen. "It has been a long, slow process to gain his confidence to the point where he would wear a harness, a necessary step toward walking him." She started out walking Copper around her property, and when he was ready, they began taking short walks around Duarte.

Copper, who will grow to six feet, enjoys his walks, and passersby certainly are excited to see him. "Once someone thought he was an ostrich," laughed Eileen. She says he always brings a smile to the faces of children and adults alike. She often hears people call out "No way!" or "What am I seeing?"

Left to right: Eileen Harrington Robinson, Copper and Sister Gaudercia of Santa Teresita. A familiar sight these days along the Royal Oaks walking trail is Eileen Robinson with Copper, a llama that belongs to a firefighter residing in Bradbury. "Copper does one thing really well," says Eileen, "he makes people smile."

Copper is a curious animal. He listens carefully and is keenly aware of everything around him. It is true that llamas occasionally spit, especially among themselves or at humans they consider to be equals. They are cousins of the camel.

It is said that llamas originated in the central plains of North America about forty million years ago before migrating to South America. The imported population of llamas in the United States and Canada numbers more than 150,000. They are one of the oldest domestic animals in the world.

Eileen brushes Copper, makes sure he always has fresh water and feeds him Bermuda grass. She is always happy to behold the love and beauty Copper radiates when people stop to enjoy him. "I like to think he belongs to everyone," says Eileen, who jokingly said she was going to ask the city council to install a "llama crossing" in town. On a recent visit to Santa Teresita Hospital, children in the day care as well as elderly residents and many of the sisters enjoyed a visit from Copper. He did what he does best—brought smiles to the faces of those who saw him.

NITA CAREY: WORKING THE POLLS EIGHTY TIMES!

November 13, 2008

Francis "Nita" Carey served as a poll worker for the eightieth time on November 4, 2008. She has served since 1952, when Eisenhower was on the ballot. She has received numerous awards, one of which was from the Los Angeles County Board of Supervisors for being the longest-serving poll worker.

When a friend called and asked if she would like to work at the local polling place, Frances "Nita" Carey thought it might be fun, so she agreed to go. Recently, Nita received recognition from the county board of supervisors for being the longest-serving poll worker in Los Angeles County. On November 4, she served for the eightieth time.

It was in 1952 and Eisenhower was on the ballot for president when Nita first performed her civic duty. Since that time, she has served countless hours as a poll worker for national, city, primary and school board elections, in addition to a small water board election held in what was then called "Rock Town." Along the way, she began working as an inspector and recalls, "In the old days, I knew everyone who came in to vote because we were a smaller town back then."

The supervisors presented her with several certificates thanking her for her dedication.

Having moved to Duarte in 1949, Nita, now eighty-three years old, was active in PTAs in the local schools and recently received a certificate for her fifty-year membership in the Duarte Woman's Club, where she once served as president and continues today to be an active member.

Looking back, Nita remembers the time when paper ballots were three to four feet long and marked with specific marking pens. She admits that she never kept track of the many times she served as a poll worker but that "they keep detailed records at the board of supervisors."

Born in San Marino, Nita was sixteen years old when she married Ed, who passed away a few years ago.

WILLIAM LANCASTER: CITY PAYS TRIBUTE TO FORMER MAYOR AND HIS VISION

March 7, 2004

"Come back with me to the 1960s," invited Diane Smith at a recent gathering. "These were the days when gas was twenty-five cents a gallon, the Ford Mustang was the hottest car to emerge and Pepsi came in glass bottles."

The audience remembered and listened intently as Smith continued, "There was a young, handsome employee of Pepsi Cola named Bill Lancaster who became a Duarte City councilman. Even in those days, he had a vision of what the growth would be in Southern California."

Smith, daughter of Bill Lancaster, was addressing an impressive group of local government officials, representatives of the California Department of Transportation, the office of Assemblyman Dennis Mountjoy and friends and family of the late Bill Lancaster.

When you drive the 210 Freeway, you will notice recently placed signs reading "William H. Lancaster Memorial Highway." These signs, one at the Mountain exit in Duarte and one just west of the I-15, were unveiled at this gathering, held February 27 at the Duarte Historical Museum in a tribute paid to this man of vision.

Bob Poff, Duarte city manager in the 1960s, recalled the days Lancaster served on the Duarte City Council and as mayor for three terms. He remembered that Lancaster was instrumental in the incorporation of Duarte (August 27, 1957) and that when the 210 Freeway was constructed, it was Lancaster who passionately fought the original plans, which contained no provision for offramp access to Duarte. In the words of Lancaster's daughter: "He lobbied hard for an offramp for the then-budding city of Duarte. He won."

Lancaster went on to serve as district representative, appointed by U.S. representative Charles Wiggens, and in 1972 was elected to the California

Assembly, where he represented major portions of the Pomona and San Gabriel Valleys. He retired in 1992 and died in 2000.

Accompanied by her brother, Chris (a West Covina councilman), Diane spoke of her father's passion and commitment to community and local government and lamented the fact that he had died before "physically witnessing the fruits of his labors."

Duarte mayor John Fasana, flanked by Councilwoman Tzeitel Paras, presented a proclamation to the Lancaster family, stating that the City of Duarte shares in "this fitting tribute to the memory of William H. 'Bill' Lancaster, and proudly recognizes his place in Duarte's rich history as one of the visionaries who led the City of Duarte to its incorporation."

It was through the efforts of Assemblyman Dennis Mountjoy's ACR 2 (Assembly Committee Resolution), which was unanimously approved and chartered by the secretary of state, that the portion of the 210 Freeway between Duarte and State Highway 15 is named the William H. Lancaster Memorial Highway.

From now on, in the words of Lancaster's daughter, when you see that sign as you drive along the 210, you will remember that Bill Lancaster was a man of vision, passion and diligence.

Kitty Kelly: A Duarte Mother Remembered

May 2012

Traditionally, Mother's Day is a time to pay tribute to the women who gave life and reared their children through their formative years. Rosemary Moreno Yull remembers her mother as a strong and dedicated woman, a courageous adventurer tempered with kindness and love.

Her mom, Kitty Kelly Moreno, arrived in Duarte in December 1944 when her husband, a chef, landed a job at Elliott's Rest Home, a tuberculosis facility on Duarte Road. While he started work in Duarte, she took care of the arrangements at their home in Bridgeport, Connecticut, and although she had never driven a car, she loaded seven-month-old Rosemary and her four siblings into the family's 1937 Packard and headed west on I-40 and then Route 66, a ten-day trip. Upon arrival, she immediately fell in love with Duarte and its fragrant odor of citrus.

Behind the street sign for Cinco Robles is the saga of the Moreno family, their unusual trip to Duarte and the courage and entrepreneurship of the matriarch, Kitty. The naming of the street was a surprise to all, and more surprises followed in the later years.

After living in several places, Kitty purchased eight acres of land in the shadow of the City of Hope. Soon the value of the property increased, and this was the beginning of her real estate career. She set out to build the family homestead on her land next to five stately oaks that she had grown to love. "She absolutely loved those oaks," says Rosemary. "Before the house was built, being postwar, supplies and money were in short supply. There were seven of us, and my mother, being so strong and positive, would not leave her 'land,' so she bought a twenty-by-twenty naval hospital tent in Monrovia in which the family lived for two years while she slowly built a house next to 'her oaks.'"

The oaks that she so loved are deeply rooted in Duarte's history. They are the same oaks for which the street Cinco Robles was named, and their roots have spread into music history. Kitty had the honor of naming the street leading to her property, and to everyone's surprise, she named it Cinco Robles. The name she selected proved to be prophetic.

"History says that a songwriter named Larry Sullivan would travel down Duarte Road on his way to work. He would pass the sign and loved the words

'Cinco Robles,'" says Rosemary "When he asked what it was about, neighbors told him that the street was named by my mother after the five oaks that grew in our yard nearby. It inspired him to write the song 'Cinco Robles,' which was recorded by Les Paul and Mary Ford." The song was performed on the Ed Sullivan, Tennessee Ernie Ford and Dinah Shore shows.

Kitty flourished as a real estate agent. Her office at the corner of Huntington Drive and Crestfield was a bright yellow building with green shamrocks and a sign that read KITTY KELLY REAL ESTATE. "As a real estate agent, my mother loved to help people purchase a first home, and she would often loan her commission to help them along," recalls Rosemary.

In 1961, Kitty sold the homestead to a philanthropist, who donated it to the City of Hope. Outpatient facilities are now on the property, and the beautiful oaks were unfortunately not spared. Rosemary and her siblings—Joseph, Richard, Thomas and Dolores (now deceased)—will always remember that home, the stately oaks and their mother, who was "a happy, self-educated woman with strong beliefs, incredible common sense, a clear vision of her family's future and the tenacity to pursue her dreams."

Kitty died in 1991 at age eighty-five in Wrightwood. Rosemary was a member of the first graduating class at Duarte High School in 1961. Her brothers graduated from MAD.

Note: Several members of the Moreno family visited Duarte for the annual Salute to Route 66 Parade in September 2012. They reunited with old friends at the pre-parade breakfast and joined in the parade. At that time, Thomas Moreno donated his Glenn Miller collection to the Duarte Museum.

GLENN MILLER: A TRIBUTE

June 2010

Although his ties with Duarte were fleeting, we feel privileged that a great man's legacy was linked with our community, if only for a short time.

Big-band leader Glenn Miller built a home on fifty-four acres of land in the shadow of the foothills in Duarte's Fish Canyon, just west of where Valley View School stands today. The year was 1941, and Miller was working on the movie *Sun Valley Serenade*. In 1942, finishing touches were made on the newly erected abode, and by then, Miller was immersed in the filming of

Bandleader Glenn Miller with his wife, Helen, in a photograph donated to the Duarte Historical Museum by Jonnie Miller, their daughter. *Courtesy of the Duarte Historical Society.*

Orchestra Wives. The opportunity to live in this foothill community with his family was inviting but short-lived.

Miller was considered the most popular bandleader in the United States, and he enjoyed this role from 1939 to 1942. He was a jazz musician,

From left to right: Truman Fisher, plaque sponsor; Richard Myer, artist; and Blake Sennett, grandson of legendary bandleader Glenn Miller, at the Glenn Miller plaque, which was unveiled on November 3, 2001, at Valley View Satellite Park (later renamed Glenn Miller Park).

arranger, composer and best-selling recording artist, but his patriotic drive trumped all of those labels. At the peak of his entertainment career, he felt compelled to join the war effort and at age thirty-eight joined the U.S. Army, at which point he took charge of an army band designed to entertain the troops and boost morale.

While his family lived in the Duarte home, Miller played the trombone for service clubs and in recreation halls in Alabama, modernizing military music—a trend that was not always well received. In the summer, Major Miller gave eight hundred performances and recorded a series of records while there, later forming a fifty-piece U.S. Army–Air Force Band, which he took to England in 1944. His band was deemed a great morale booster and a boon to the war effort. Sadly, one fateful day as he traveled from England to France to entertain troops, Miller's plane disappeared, and he was never heard from again.

The Miller family remained in Duarte for a time. His wife and two children were joined by the maternal grandparents, who came here from Colorado by train. They helped run the Miller Ranch, which included citrus and avocado orchards, strawberry fields and beehives. Miller's two small children never really knew their father.

Several years ago, the Duarte Historical Museum honored Miller by erecting a bronze plaque in the satellite park just east of his former ranch, a project spearheaded by the late Truman Fisher, a former music professor at Pasadena City College. The bronze plaque was created by Richard Myer, the same artist responsible for the Andres Duarte statue that stands on Huntington Drive today.

After the dedication of the plaque at a ceremony punctuated by a performance by a military band, the park was renamed Glenn Miller Park. The Glenn Miller home was sold in 1954, and the ranch acreage was developed into housing. In the fire that swept through the foothills above Duarte in 1980, the Miller house was destroyed.

The permanent Glenn Miller exhibit at the museum contains an array of Glenn Miller memorabilia, including several items donated by his son at the time of his visit. A painting of the home by artist Richard Myer and an architectural rendering of the Miller Ranch created by Von Haws and Michelle Miner of San Jose are also displayed.

Many Duarteans seem to be unaware of Glenn Miller's Duarte connection. And others, especially our youth, ask, "Who is Glenn Miller?"

A Slice of Big-Band Era Plays on in Duarte

November 16, 2006

"It was a real homecoming," says Steve Miller, sixty-three, who recently visited Duarte along with two of his longtime buddies who are also from the area. All three are retired Monrovia police officers. Steve, who as a toddler lived for a short time in the Fish Canyon home built by his father, the famed big-band leader Glenn Miller, toured the sight of his old home that was destroyed by fire in 1980 and visited the exhibit at the Duarte Historical Museum dedicated to the father he never really knew.

Presently living in Las Vegas, Steve and his friends reunited to celebrate the retirement of a Monrovia police chief who "I broke in when he was just a rookie," says Steve. They took this opportunity to reminisce.

Steve, John Mills and Barney Mondrala visited their old haunts, touring the sites of such long-gone places as Lyons Pony Express Museum in Arcadia, the Red Car Line "Y," Carpenters Drive In, the Big Sky Drive In, Burger Lane and Bob's Big Boy.

Steve's memories of living in Duarte are few, as he was only a small child at that time. But he grew up not far away, and his career with the Monrovia Police Department kept him in the area.

After his father's disappearance, Steve's maternal grandparents came to Duarte by train from Boulder, Colorado, to oversee the ranch, which included citrus and avocado orchards, strawberry fields and beehives raising honey for Honeyville. In 1946, Steve and his sister Jonnie came "to the wilds of Duarte" with their mother and lived on the ranch until she bought a home in San Marino.

The Duarte home sold in 1954, and the ranch acreage was replaced by housing. Steve will be supplementing the Duarte Museum's Glenn Miller exhibit with memorabilia and photographs. "The house in Fish Canyon was really for band practice, and it was my father's plan to have a permanent home built when he returned home from the war," Steve notes. Steve will be donating a hand sketch his father made of the home he had hoped to build for the family.

RAY BRADBURY: HONORARY DUARTEAN

June 12, 2012

There are worse crimes than burning books. One of them is not reading them.
—Ray Bradbury

If ever there were an "honorary Duartean," it would be the late Ray Bradbury. One of America's most honored and beloved authors, Bradbury did not wait for an invitation to grace our town with his presence. He took it upon himself to send a congratulatory letter to Peter Rosenwald, community library manager at the time, who had just received the Golden Apple Award from the Duarte School District. At that time, Bradbury offered to give a local fundraising talk and book signing, an offer that was graciously accepted. In 2002, before a record crowd at the Duarte PAC Center, his eloquent and heartfelt talk was well received. He had won the hearts of Duarteans.

Bradbury rejected remuneration for his appearance, and monies made from the book sales were used to support the Duarte Library. According to Mary Somerlott, Duarte City publicist, "He was as inspiring a speaker as

Mary Barrow Somerlott, Duarte's publicist, sits with Ray Bradbury. The author, playwright and lecturer visited Duarte several times, giving talks and participating in the annual Festival of Authors. He donated proceeds from his talks and book sales to the Friends of the Duarte Library. *Courtesy of Mary Barrow Somerlott.*

I have ever heard. He delighted in sharing the story of his life and of his writing and expressed such joy and love of both." At the conclusion of his talk, he remained for two hours, signing books and answering questions. "He had just turned eighty, and his energy was amazing," Somerlott added. October 5, 2002, was proclaimed "Ray Bradbury Day" in Duarte by the City of Duarte and the Friends of the Duarte Library.

Bradbury returned to Duarte in 2005 at a time when the local One Town, One Book project featured as its reading selection Bradbury's *The Martian Chronicles*. "Again he packed the PAC Center, gave his talk, answered questions and signed hundreds of books," recalls Somerlott.

To include the younger crowd, the project also featured Bradbury's *Switch on the Night*, a picture book about a boy who conquers his fear of the night. Bradbury was delighted, saying, "This book is very special to me. I wrote it four months before our first child was born. When I was a little boy, I was afraid of the dark. I didn't want my child to be afraid, so I wrote a book that I could read to her and later on she could read to herself."

Bradbury returned to Duarte in 2007, 2008 and 2009 as a speaker at the annual Festival of Authors. He was a lover of libraries and summed up that love as follows: "When I graduated from high school in 1938, I began going to the library three nights a week. I did this every week for almost ten years, and finally, in 1947, about the time I got married, I figured I was done. I had graduated from the library."

Bradbury has written more than five hundred published works, including short stories, novels, plays, screenplays, TV scripts and verse. Among his other well-known novels are *Something Wicked This Way Comes*, *The Halloween Tree*, *The Illustrated Man*, *The October Country*, *Dandelion Wine* and, of course, *Fahrenheit 451*. He was unable to attend the most recent Festival of Authors because his health had declined. He died on June 5, 2012, and will be missed by his loving Duarte fans.

Author Roderick Thorp (September 1, 1936–April 28, 1999) Lived Quietly While His Words Roared

May 19, 1999

Although he was the author of best-selling detective novels, few Duarteans knew he lived among us. Roderick Thorp, who died recently at the age of sixty-two, moved to Duarte in 1989 and worked quietly from his home. I met him in 1992 while he was researching *The Green River Killings*, based on a series of unsolved murders in Washington.

I was a novice columnist with the paper when I asked Thorp for an interview. He agreed, asking me to meet him in the bar at Conrad's (now Denny's). This seemed a bit odd, but moments after meeting the author, I felt at ease. He was kind, straightforward and humble. Later, he admitted he only agreed to the interview because I have the same first name as his wife.

Thorp recounted his entrance into the writing world. He tried to enroll in a creative writing class at City College of New York but was told by the professor that he didn't have the skills to succeed. However, he was determined, and his perseverance paid off. Several months and many writings later, the same professor dubbed him "a diamond in the rough."

In the ensuing years, Thorp published several novels, selling movie rights to many of them. Probably his most popular novel is *Nothing Lasts Forever*, to which Fox bought the movie rights in 1987 and changed the title to *Die Hard*. Released in 1988, the movie grossed $86 million domestically and enjoyed success abroad and in the video market. Thorp's characters lived on in the *Die Hard* sequels.

Thorp's passion for writing began in his childhood. He recalled reading a stack of comic books and deciding he wanted to write stories. He followed the advice he gave other aspiring writers: "Write every day and don't give up."

Although Thorp was reared in New York and lived in such intriguing places as Chelsea, England, and the French Riviera, he loved living in Duarte, citing its simplicity and friendliness. "I love the sounds of life that echo around my neighborhood," he told me, "the children playing rollerblade hockey in the street and the everyday sounds of suburbia."

Working at home all day, Thorp joked that he was a key player in the neighborhood watch program. Thorp published more than a dozen works, ten of them novels. Some were not appreciated by the public. During the 1960s, returning to Los Angeles from a long stay in Europe, he was distressed by what he considered an overwhelming drug problem in this country, especially the use of cocaine. After much research, he published a book with Harper & Row entitled *The Music of Their Laughter*, which featured a series of interviews on the threat of drugs in U.S. high schools and how drugs get to the States from South America. This work met with great resistance.

"People didn't want to hear about the drug threat at that time," said Thorp. His book was published too early to be taken seriously. Other novels published by Thorp are *The Detective*, published in 1966 and released years later as a movie starring Frank Sinatra; *Rainbow Drive* in 1966, dealing with the infamous Laurel Canyon murders, which became a Showtime movie; and *Devlin*, a story about New York cops.

Thorp is survived by his wife, Claudia, sons Roddy and Stephen and grandchildren Stacey, Valerie and Carolyn. He lived a quiet but exciting life, and his many stories—fiction and nonfiction—will keep his memory alive.

The Tracks of Jill Miller Story

September 1, 2001

A heartwarming story about a mostly forgotten episode in Duarte's history was brought to light recently in a most surprising place. The current issue of *Classic Trains* magazine featured a story written by Jack Elwood entitled "The Little White Frame House by the Tracks," and with the publisher's generous permission, I wish to share this article with you.

Jill Miller was eighteen years old in 1950, when this saga unfolds. Bedridden with rheumatic fever, her contact with the outside world had diminished to the point that her life revolved around the sound of passing trains. Jill lived on Duarte Road near the railroad tracks that run across the street from the City of Hope. In 1950, Santa Fe ran five passenger trains each way daily on the Second District. To pass the time in her quiet, lonely world, Jill would wave a small flag back and forth through an opening in her window each time she heard a train passing by.

In most instances, this act would go unnoticed, but as fate would have it, according to the article, O.D. "Orrie" Kelly, a veteran regular engineer on Train 20, the *Chief*, noticed the flag waving and became curious. He checked with other crew members to see if they knew anything about the little white frame house and the "flag waver," but no one knew a thing.

The article admits that "railroad men" have the general reputation of being "cranky, macho types," and this was apparently true about Kelly. But something must have pulled at his heartstrings, because one day after returning the locomotive to the Redondo Junction Roundhouse in Los Angeles, he returned by car to the little house in Duarte, home of the flag waver. It was there that the mother introduced him to Jill, and a long-lasting friendship between Jill, Kelly and dozens of train crew members began to blossom.

The story of Jill Miller soon spread throughout the railroad, and through Kelly, monetary collections poured in from all points and every department. As Christmas neared, the crews collected gifts for Jill and even bought her a recliner chair and television set, "a relative rarity in those days." After obtaining permission from Santa Fe management to stop the eastbound *Chief* opposite the house, the crew unloaded the gifts and carried them across Duarte Road, delivering them to Jill.

As time went on, Jill's story was told in an *L.A. Times* article, following which the Railway Club of Southern California befriended her. When she was able to leave her house, the club sponsored an excursion train to San Diego with Jill as the guest of honor. "Thus did the 'Jill Miller Holiday' special come about on Sunday, October 28, 1951." Santa Fe Diesel No. 167 led the ten-car train to San Diego with an all-volunteer crew on board.

Although the San Diego–bound special originated in Los Angeles, it first headed out to Monrovia so that Jill could board at her nearest station. She was set up in a room in the Pullman car in which Santa Fe had provided a courier nurse to accompany and assist her. It was reportedly a wonderful trip for Jill, fulfilling her wish to see the Pacific Ocean.

Despite pessimistic reports from Jill's doctors, she gained back her health and graduated from high school. Her friendship with the train crews persevered, and in time, she fell in love with Harold Bussy, a young engineer. The couple married and moved to San Bernardino. As time went on, Bussy died, but Jill later remarried and today, at the age of seventy-nine, lives in Los Angeles.

Many thanks to Kalmbach Publishers for permission to share this story. A copy of the magazine with the complete article and photos is available to read at the Duarte Historical Museum library.

DUARTE LOSES LONGTIME RESIDENT LOUISE WINKLER

October 15, 2006

Her home was as much a part of her as she was a part of Duarte. Louise Oliver Winkler, a sixty-two-year resident of Duarte, died of natural causes at the age of ninety-eight on the morning of October 2. She died in the same house, the same room and the same bed in which her mother passed away in 1948. It was the way she wanted it.

In 1944, Louise and her husband, Adrian, headed west, traveling along Old Route 66 from Maple Hill, Kansas, to Monrovia, where Adrian operated a gas station and auto repair shop. In 1946, they purchased a circa 1880 home on Royal Oaks Drive in Duarte they called Shady Oaks that encompasses three acres of land, including an avocado orchard. There they raised four sons: David, Richard, Lawrence and Kent. Reminiscing about those days, Louise once confided to me that one of her fondest memories was the sound of a ball bouncing against the house. "That sound was comforting," she said, "because I knew my boys were home, playing together and having fun." The sound would prompt her to head for the kitchen to bake up a batch of cookies.

Chris Feldman, the first American Field Exchange student in Duarte, made his home with the Winklers for the 1965–66 school year.

After Adrian died in 2000, Louise kept his home office exactly as he had left it. And although their sons grew up and moved away, the boys returned home often, taking turns with the household chores and upkeep, enabling Louise to remain there. "She didn't want to leave," says her son Dave. "She loved the home and wouldn't leave it."

Louise was a volunteer in Duarte throughout her life. She officially became a member of St. Luke's Episcopal Church in Monrovia in 1945. She was involved with all facets of church life, according to Steve Baker, Monrovia-Duarte historian and Winkler family friend. "For over thirty-five years, Louise volunteered with the St. Luke's Economy Shop, an outreach effort founded by Alyce Kelly to provide members of the community with limited incomes to shop, with dignity, for good, used items," says Baker.

Louise was also active in the Duarte Reading Circle, the Garden Club and the Home Chapter of the City of Hope, and for years she served as a docent at the Duarte Historical Museum. "The Winklers had become firmly woven into the fabric of my life," says Baker. "Occasionally, I will sit quietly in the empty church at St. Luke's and allow the memories of past years to come flooding back. I can see, with my mind's eye, the faces of those who once occupied the pews around me but now belong to another congregation. Louise has joined that congregation, and I will never forget her."

DUARTEANS WHO LEFT A MARK

They were familiar faces around town, helping to shape Duarte's future and playing an active part in community projects. Then, for a variety of reasons, they moved on, with life in Duarte but a memory.

Bob and Julie Davey

For thirty-three years, Bob and Julie Davey made their home in Duarte, both highly regarded as friends and dedicated volunteers. They are among those visionaries who shaped Duarte's future. Bob was voted onto the city council in 1995 and served as mayor in 1999. Julie, a retired Fullerton College professor, spent countless volunteer hours teaching Writing for Wellness classes at the City of Hope. The Daveys moved to Laguna Niguel in 2009, although they often return for special events.

Authors Bob and Julie Davey were Duarte activists, sponsoring a number of community projects. Julie was a volunteer at the City of Hope, teaching a class in "Wellness through Writing." Bob pilots his Mooney, flying patients to their treatments. The couple recently moved to Laguna Niguel. *Courtesy of the Daveys.*

Bob, a pilot who owns a Mooney airplane, continues his third year with Angel Flights, a national organization that transports needy cancer patients to receive medical treatment. Bob is among seven thousand pilots who not only donate their time and airplanes to this charitable cause but also absorb the cost of gasoline. In a sense coming home, he has flown out-of-state children to the City of Hope. Julie continues to teach her writing class, now at Mission Hospital.

As for their life in Duarte, Julie says, "We made wonderful lifetime friends and look upon our days there with fondness for the people and all of the volunteers who give their time and talent to make it a wonderful city."

Rae Gordon

When Rae Gordon left town several years ago, her many friends in the Duarte Woman's Club and the Rancho Duarte Garden Club were saddened. She was the quiet force behind her late husband, Otis Gordon, after whom a Duarte sports field is named. Rae's friends always looked down on her due to the fact she was barely four feet tall. Despite her small size, she was a big volunteer and was active, along with Otis, in the move during the 1950s to incorporate the city.

For the past several years, Rae has been living at a senior home in San Clemente. Her daughter Gerri reports that at age ninety-seven, Rae is doing well and keeps up with Duarte news in the local papers.

Note: Rae Gordon died on January 18, 2012.

Rae Gordon (left) and Helen Vaughan. These ladies were deeply embedded in Duarte life. Rae was an active member of the Duarte Woman's Club, the Duarte Reading Circle and the Rancho de Duarte Garden Club. Helen was, for many years, the Duarte librarian. Promoting literacy was her passion.

Helen Vaughan

Helen Vaughan was a strong supporter of literacy, a lover of classical music and an avid enthusiast for all ecological endeavors. Her Duarte connection came when she began working for the Los Angeles County Library System in 1968 and was later an in-charge librarian for Baldwin Park and Duarte Libraries. Those who knew her considered her a Duartean because she was deeply involved in the fabric of this town. Literacy was one of her chief passions, and working at libraries gave her the opportunity to encourage others of all ages to embrace knowledge through reading.

A lover of history, Helen was a dedicated member of the Duarte Historical Society, serving as the organization's secretary for many years. She was also an enthusiastic member of the Duarte Garden Club, the San Gabriel Rose Society, the Reading Circle and the Nature Conservancy. When the library could not afford to hire a "children's librarian," she took over those duties as well. She possessed the ability to teach children about the importance of reading, disguising the lessons with parties, teas or special celebrations.

Even in her advanced age, Helen continued to expand her mind, recently studying such subjects as the universe and geology.

Note: Helen died on February 19, 2012.

Loyd Gibbons

Loyd's Bike Shop is a good example of what makes this town special. Since 1985, Loyd Gibbons has served as a guru to classic bicycle enthusiasts, repairing their coveted vintage Schwinns with an endless cache of parts. His small building on Highland Avenue just south of Royal Oaks Drive is overflowing with bikes and trikes, wheels, tires, Tonka trucks and memorabilia. Indeed, you need to pick a path to negotiate through. But the man knows what is where!

Loyd explains that Schwinn went out of business in 1986, and nowadays, the bikes are made by another company. Although he repairs and sells a variety of bikes, overhauling original Schwinns is his passion. Neighborhood kids drop in with broken bikes that were bought elsewhere, "but I like to help them out by fixing or adjusting their bikes for free," says Loyd.

Indeed, his shop is much more than just a bike shop. Former mayor Lois Gaston recalls, "My adult sons still talk about going there and getting advice about how to succeed in life, in addition to how to keep their bikes repaired."

Loyd's Duarte roots run deep. He arrived in town in 1965, and his shop, which was first in Monrovia, has anchored the present spot since 1985. Negotiating through the rows of bikes, he pointed me to a rear wall that sported a plaque he had received as president of the Duarte Kiwanis in 1972. "I was the first black president of the organization," he said.

Trailing closely behind his passion for bicycles is his talent as a musician, singing and playing the saxophone. "I still do some one-nighters," he said. He has pursued his musical talents since working in the business during the 1940s. When asked his age, he grinned and replied that his birth parents are Cherokee Indian and that "Indians never give their age."

Jan and Bob Wight

Jan and Bob Wight were among the local movers and shakers of Duarte during its pivotal years. Jan served on the Duarte School Board from 1983 to 1995 and as president in 1987, 1990, 1991 and 1995. She later served as president/CEO of the Duarte Chamber of Commerce from 1995 to 2008. Bob served on both the Duarte Cable Commission and Planning

Jan and Bob Wight were, for many years, among the movers and shakers of Duarte.

Commission and was president of the Duarte Kiwanis. He currently is the business manager for the Foothill Unity Center. Jan is now retired.

The couple has moved to Azusa, and although both are dealing with health issues, they return to Duarte often to shop and see friends. Jan says:

> *I value and treasure my years of service to Duarte. It was an exciting time to see Duarte grow, prosper and put itself on the map. I am delighted to have had a part in that and to have worked with the many creative and dedicated people who made Duarte our kind of town. I still go to Duarte to purchase goods or services whenever I can, and I love seeing people I have known all these years.*

Ruth Gardner: The Energizer Bunny

November 17, 2002

She was all that was good and positive in Duarte, a shining example to young and old. The recent death of Ruth Gardner has left us asking, "Why did she die so young?" Okay, she died just shy of her ninety-fourth birthday, but her energy, impeccable appearance and kindness to all radiated a youthfulness that women half her age envied and respected.

A smile and kind word were always on her lips. When she volunteered to bring punch to an event, she would defy her slight frame by lugging her crystal punch bowl and would shun offers of cubed ice, insisting on making an "ice ring."

Ruth considered Duarte's campaign to win "All-America City" status as a highlight in her life. She traveled to Louisville to represent our town. "She never realized her age, and if she did, she never let it stop her," says city council member Margaret Finlay. "In Louisville, she was the one who got up early and urged us to practice our routine for the judges. I admired her spunk and good nature."

Ruth Gardner (November 16, 1908–November 17, 2001). One of Duarte's most active volunteers, Ruth's daughters called her the "Energizer Bunny."

An active member of no fewer than a dozen local community service organizations, Ruth attended activities, often with her daughters, Jeanne and Linda, at her side. They affectionately referred to their mother as the "Energizer Bunny." Her involvement began in 1952 when she moved to Duarte from Pasadena. She campaigned in favor of incorporating our town and worked to secure an offramp for Duarte when the 210 Freeway was in planning stages. A new location for the library and better schools were her next causes. After finishing a Red Cross course, Ruth began working at blood banks, an activity she employed to the end.

We mourn a loss that leaves us with the fondest of memories about a lady we all admired.

JANNA VEE MATHAS'S LITERACY LEGACY

Family, friends and a passion for writing and storytelling are the legacy of Janna Vee Mathas, affectionately called by her middle name, Vee. She left Virginia in 1946 in a convertible driven by her future husband, William, and arrived in Duarte along Route 66. In her recent death, she left our community a better place through her commitment to volunteerism and sharing of the written word. Three of the Mathas children graduated from Duarte High School: Dorothy in 1965, William in 1967 and Timothy in 1970. The youngest, Carla, graduated from Alverno.

"She never tired of entertaining with her amusing stories and imaginative mind," says Carla.

Fittingly, Vee served as the society editor for the local newspaper, the *Duartean*, for eleven years. She operated a local printing business, worked for both the Visiting Nurses Association and Rubio Canyon Land and Water Association and still found time to do volunteer work.

BELOVED BETSY BACON

January 22, 2009

Betsy Bacon (November 24, 1921–December 26, 2008). Born into a Duarte pioneer family, Betsy graduated from Monrovia-Arcadia-Duarte (MAD) High School in 1939, traveled the world and returned home to teach in Duarte schools. Duarte's Tocino Drive is named after her family. *Courtesy of the Bacon family.*

The fabric of Duarte is missing a stitch with the recent death of Betsy Bacon. She was one of a kind—a teacher, world traveler, athlete and daughter of one of Duarte's most prominent pioneer families. Her grandfather, Captain Williamson Ware Bacon Sr., his wife, Elizabeth, daughter Elizabeth and sons W.W. Jr. and Robert came to Duarte from Kentucky in 1888 and at that time were portrayed as the "epitome of the Southern upper class," according to *On the Duarte*.

Captain Bacon was described as a "slender, erect gentleman of great dignity wrapped around a whimsical sense of humor," and his wife was tall, willowy, ethereal and beautiful. She also had a sense of humor. Those who knew Betsy would certainly agree that she took after her grandparents in many ways. She was born on November 24, 1921, to W.W. "Bill" and Jacqueline "Lide" Bacon. A few years later came her sister, Jacqueline, who presently resides at Westminster Gardens.

The family lived on "The Ranch," a two-story California home that prior to being rebuilt in 1913 was the original old adobe home erected by Andres Avelino Duarte, the town's namesake. Today, a portion of the old adobe still stands incorporated within the large walk-in pantry in the kitchen. The property was subdivided in the mid-1960s, and only the Bacon family name remains in the form of Tocino Drive (*tocino* is the Spanish word for bacon).

Betsy graduated from Monrovia-Arcadia-Duarte High School in 1939, went on to Occidental College and earned her master's degree at Columbia University in New York. For many years, she taught in Saudi Arabia, Japan and England, traveling to scores of other countries during school vacations. Returning to Duarte in the 1960s, Betsy taught at Maxwell, Andres Duarte and Northview until she retired.

Betsy was an athletic figure and had many interests. She belonged to the Monrovia Tennis Club, the Van Baake Ski Club and the Santa Anita Wood Carvers and served as a counselor at a girls' camp in Big Bear. For many years, she was a member of the Monrovia Garden Club and served as a docent at the Duarte Historical Museum. She was a lifetime member of the Monrovia Presbyterian Church, where her memorial services were held.

Jacqueline will always remember Besty as "a good big sister who always looked after me."

Note: Betsy died on December 26, 2008.

OTIS GORDON SPORTS PARK—THE MAN BEHIND THE SIGN

September 1994

As future generations enjoy Duarte's newest project, the Otis Gordon Sports Park, what will they know of the man behind the sign?

At age eighty-five, Gordon is as active today as he was in 1952 when he and his wife, Rae, made Duarte their home. With children in the local schools, Gordon immediately became active in the PTA and received a lifetime membership. His community spirit grew, and he joined the Duarte

Otis Gordon was an activist who worked diligently to improve the quality of life in Duarte. His many projects remain part of our town today. The Otis Gordon Sports Park is located on Central Avenue next to Andres Duarte School. *Courtesy of the Gordon family.*

Citizen's Association, where he served as president and helped form the Sanitation District in 1954 to bring sewer lines to Duarte.

His work continued as he championed the passing of a school bond to build a new high school. The issue was defeated three times, a result that he blamed on Monrovia school board members. Gordon then became the suspected instigator of a rumor that if the bond failed a fourth time, a boycott of Monrovia businesses would occur. The bond then passed. That year, he served as emcee at the opening ceremonies of the new Duarte Library.

In 1956, Gordon's crusade was the fight for the incorporation of the City of Duarte. "After months of hard work, with Azusa, Bradbury and Monrovia fighting us all the way, we were finally incorporated on August 22, 1957," recalls Gordon. "Working with the chamber of commerce, I was in charge of the installation ceremonies held at Andres Duarte School, where a municipal court judge swore in the candidates."

Not one to sit back and digest success, Gordon became involved in a series of civic projects. He remained active in the chamber and in 1959 served as president of the first Duarte Parade and Fiesta. He was elected to the city council in 1960 and was co-chairman of a recall committee in a successful effort to recall a council member who was sentenced for shoplifting.

Many of Gordon's efforts flourish today, such as the formation of the City Beautification Committee and the Rancho Duarte Garden Club. He steadfastly opposed a proposal to introduce poker parlors within the city borders, a proposition that was defeated.

Gordon speaks most fondly of a project he undertook involving the display of American flags along the Huntington median. Despite what he describes as a negative response from the city, Gordon hired a blacksmith to create a flag holder for a median pole, mounted a flag and took a photo. "Armed with the photo and an explanation, I presented the plan to the managers of the telephone company and Edison," he recalls. "In time, the project was approved, and I turned it over to our Armed Forces for implementation." Soon Duarte was called the "City of Flags."

Gordon may move more slowly these days, but he still possesses a quick wit and strong desire to champion any cause he feels will improve the quality of life in Duarte. It is fitting that the park will bear his name.

Note: Otis Gordon passed away in 1997.

VIRGINIA DELFINA ARMENTA DE LOS REYES SCHMAHL

June 24, 2010

Just shy of her 100th birthday, Virginia Delfina Armenta de los Reyes Schmahl is looking forward to a family reunion in her honor. Born on June 25, 1910, in Sonora, Mexico, she vividly recalls the events that shaped her life.

Her father was employed by Jose de la Cruz Porfirio Diaz Mori, who served as president of Mexico from 1876 to 1911. During the revolution, Virginia and her family fled to the United States for their safety. They lived in San Diego for a while and eventually moved to her maternal grandfather's home in Los Angeles, which at the time was farmland.

Virginia was educated in both Mexico and the United States, and upon completion of her education, she worked as an international telephone operator for the phone company. According to her daughter-in-law, Joanne Schmahl, Virginia's favorite pastimes were dancing and playing musical instruments such as guitar and piano. She worked as a seamstress in both the garment and upholstery industries, was married and raised three children. She moved to Duarte in 1971 with her husband, Frederick, who served in the U.S. Army during World War II. "Duarte looked a lot different back then," she recalls.

After years of volunteer work both at the Duarte Senior Center and in the apartment complex where she lives, she is now "taking it easy." She says she used to love teaching English to Spanish-speaking residents, telling them it is never too late to learn. "My mother remained energetic and independent well into her nineties," says Virginia's sixty-six-year-old son Joseph. "It wasn't unusual for her to hop onto a bus and travel out of state to visit friends or relatives."

The stories of her early life have been passed down and remain in the hearts of her children. "Her great-grandfather came to California during the gold rush to dig for his fortune. He settled down in Los Angeles and owned a ranch where the civic center lies today," relates Joseph.

Virginia took her oath of allegiance and became a United States citizen in 1997. "It was one of the proudest moments of her life," says Joanne.

In Joanne's words, Virginia has lived through the Roaring Twenties and the First and Second World Wars. She still marvels at the many changes she has witnessed in her lifetime, from the horse-and-buggy to the automobile, from the Wright brothers to space travel.

Over one hundred family members and friends will gather to celebrate her birthday this weekend.

Note: The family of Ms. Schmahl sadly reports that she passed away peacefully on October 17, 2010, at the age of 101.

BOB DAVEY: TAKING TO THE SKIES WITH AN EYE ON DUARTE

January 22, 2006

He was a five-year-old child, poking around where he wasn't supposed to be, when he discovered an "old busted model airplane" that belonged to his father. That find by Bob Davey blossomed into a love for building model planes, which in turn fueled a passion for flying.

Growing up in Brooklyn, Davey entered model airplane competitions throughout his school years, so it isn't surprising that he later graduated from the Air Force Academy. Receiving pilot training in the U.S. Air Force, he became an instructor pilot. Earning his doctorate in aeronautics at Cal Tech, Davey joined the Aero Club and enjoyed flying small planes, which he often rented for personal use.

In 1952, he married his wife, Julie, and in 1974, the couple purchased their first plane, a Piper single-engine four-seater, which offered an

Bob Davey served as Duarte mayor in 1998–99. He graduated from the Air Force Academy and worked as a flight instructor. His passion for flying led Davey and his wife, Julie, to buy a Mooney, and the couple frequently takes off into the sky.

opportunity for adventures throughout the nation. "Mostly we like to fly to national parks and then hike," says Davey. The couple moved to Duarte in 1979, and Bob served as mayor from 1998 to 1999. In 1988, the couple bought a Mooney that was recently awarded "Best Mooney Type 201" by the Mooney Aircraft Pilots Association.

It was a clear December morning when I waved so long to my husband, Alan, who was joining Davey in his Mooney to photograph Route 66 from the air, taking off from El Monte and landing for lunch at the airport in Kingman, Arizona. The highlight of the trip was photographing Duarte, especially our neighborhood in Fish Canyon. The flight was a milestone for Alan, who has traveled many times along the western portions of Route 66 and even explored the flip side of the Mother Road touring a gold mine near Oatman, Arizona, that navigates along a tunnel under Route 66. Now he could boast that he had been on, under and over the famed highway.

JEAN EWING-SCOTT GREENE: RESIDENT WRITES UNIQUE LIFE STORY

November 14, 2004

A familiar face around town is Duartean Jean Ewing-Scott Greene, eighty-three, accompanied by her guide dog, Mazie May. Although totally blind, Jean is extremely independent and self-reliant, a fact that is not surprising given her unique, exciting and courageous life story, the details of which are chronicled in her recent book *The Men in My Life*.

Born in Chicago, Jean graduated from Northwestern University with a degree in bio-analytical chemistry. She was married to her high school sweetheart and raising two young daughters when tragedy struck. An auto accident took the lives of her family, and in an instant, she became "a childless widow."

In 1951, while working three jobs, Jean was assigned to supervise an ambulance crew at the 500 Mile Race in Indianapolis. While on duty, a roof collapsed, trapping seventy victims beneath the rubble. "I used common sense and make-do methods," said Jean, who jumped in and supervised the rescue effort. Amazingly, only one victim died. Her quick response was publicized in the news, and shortly thereafter, Jean was shocked to be summoned to the United Nations in New York by then Secretary General Dag Hammarskjold. At his urging, she accepted a position in which she would organize a unit of people and equipment that could be dispatched immediately when a disaster occurred anywhere in the world.

For the next thirty-two years, Jean traveled all over the world, mainly to third-world countries, to supervise her handpicked crew in the search and rescue of victims of such disasters as floods, earthquakes, hurricanes and monsoons. She traveled by foot, airplane, bus, tractor, elephant, bicycle and helicopter and, in her career, made more than five hundred parachute jumps. "Actually, they weren't jumps—they were pushes," she admitted.

Her job took her to such areas as Sri Lanka, Burma, Rangoon, Manila, Java, Kuala Lumpur, Rome, Istanbul, Athens and South Africa. Along the way, she fought for human rights and against racial prejudice, and she personally rendered humanitarian aid whenever she was able.

Jean's book explains how she selected the seventy-two men from fifty-nine countries who spoke more than one hundred languages and dialects. They were doctors, engineers, underwater salvage operators, pilots and radiomen. For thirty-two years, they were her family.

After retiring, she traveled around the United States in a Volkswagen van, pursing her newfound passion for oil painting. Finally, she settled down in Monrovia and then moved to Duarte because she "liked the attitude of the people."

But again, her life took a sharp turn. Four years ago, she became totally blind. Today, she lives with her seeing-eye dog, Mazie May. Her book was published this year, and she has already begun penning a new book to be entitled *The Confessions of a Guide Dog*. Jean visits local classrooms to introduce students to Mazie May and teach them about how guide dogs aid the blind. "People around town all know Mazie May," she tells me. Then she whispers out loud, "Who loves you?" and Mazie May ambles over and licks her face.

Note: A few years following my interview, Jean passed away. I attempted to check some of the "facts" in her book but was unable to confirm them. Jean's accounting of her life makes a compelling book, but whether it is fact or fiction remains to be seen.

MARY BARROW SOMERLOTT: DUARTE'S PUBLICIST AND A FOUNTAIN OF IDEAS

October 19, 2003

It always starts out the same way—her jaw drops, her eyes open wide and then she points a finger to her red hair. This is when family and friends stand back and say, "Uh oh, Mary has an idea!"

Serving as the publicist for Duarte for more than six years, Mary Barrow Somerlott keeps the public apprised of what is going on around town and is often the catalyst for community events. There is a blurry line between her volunteer work and the hours on contract when it comes to local activities and programs that affect the quality of life of a cross section of our city's residents. For example, her creative mind began to churn one day as she drove on the 605 Freeway, looking at all the billboards. Soon she had talked the billboard company into a *gratis* message, and then she coined what is today a local household phrase: "Duarte, My Kind of Town."

The billboard came and went, but the phrase remains our city's slogan. Similarly, there was a time when Mary became fed up with all the negative press about young people, especially students. It was around the time of the

Mary Barrow Somerlott is often described as the "Heart of Duarte." She has coined many community phrases, the most popular of which is "Duarte: My Kind of Town." She is the city's publicist, volunteers as a host on DCTV and is an active member of the annual Festival of Authors Committee.

Columbine tragedy that she began asking herself, "Are we doing enough for our young people—are we missing the signs?"

Her research revealed that Duarte was making youth a priority but perhaps there were residents who were not aware of the programs available. And so she organized the first local Youth Fair, declaring, "Duarte Is a Kid's Kind of Town, Too," and the day was a great success. Families learned about a variety of programs including sports, drama, reading, SAT prep, library projects, scholarship opportunities and other city-sponsored programs. City staff members volunteered their time. "It is what you can do on a shoestring when the good people of Duarte pitch in," Somerlott said. The project took on a life of its own, and this year, the fifth annual Youth Fair was held.

Somerlott has worked for KTLA/Golden West Broadcasters as director of corporate communications and handled publicity for Gene Autry's radio and television productions. Her ties with the broadcasting world are a great help in her local work today. She has been a member of the Route 66 Parade Committee since its inception and has arranged for all of the grand marshals.

Fearing the loss of the last drive-in theater on California's Route 66, Mary helped organize a joint project with Azusa volunteers that culminated in a fundraiser for Azusa's Parade Committee, the Duarte Historical Museum and DCTV. Landing a copy of the original movie *The Blob* for a showing, Mary's organizational skills and volunteer hours were responsible for another local night to remember.

For more than ten years, Mary has been an active member of DCTV, Duarte's Public Access Channel, serving as president for most of that time. She has produced dozens of human interest and historical shows, always with the aim of promoting community pride and unity. She has served on the Community Service Commission and as president of the Duarte Chamber of Commerce in 1993 and 1994.

In collaboration with artist Mark Wood, Mary has spearheaded many projects, including "People on the Bus," which resulted in colorful murals on city buses; the creative flags that adorn the median on Huntington Drive; the recent Festival of Authors, which she helped organize along with the Friends of the Library; and the One Town, One Book Committee.

Mary is not just the city's publicist; in many ways, she is Duarte's heart and soul.

Mary Blowers Lister: Heralding the Herolds

April 5, 2007

Mary Blowers was passionate about volunteer work and teaching, but she also had an adventuresome side, which she satisfied with snow skiing, water skiing, riding the air currents in hot air balloons and camping. She actively pursued her dreams until she was diagnosed with a rare, fatal disease that took her life just before Christmas 2006 at the age of seventy-one.

Like many families at the time, the Herolds left their New Jersey farm in 1948 and traveled west in search of a mild climate that would heal their young son's asthma. Unfortunately, the boy died soon after they arrived, but his sister, Mary, thrived in their new environment and over the years made her mark in Pasadena, Monrovia and Duarte.

Making their home in the Monrovia-Duarte area, the Herold family fell in love with the citrus orchards and knew they were here to stay. Mary graduated from Immaculate Conception and Monrovia High School and received her master's degree at Pasadena City College (PCC), where she taught until she retired. She was a member of dozens of clubs on the PCC campus and in Pasadena, Arcadia, Monrovia and Duarte, including the Lady Elks of Arcadia, several garden clubs, the Duarte Woman's Club, the Duarte Historical Society, several senior centers and reading circles and coin clubs.

Last year, even as her pain was advanced and her stamina waning, Mary attempted to attend community events. Wheelchair bound, she remained upbeat, dressing impeccably and managing a big smile and hearty laugh. Together with her longtime friend Duartean Brian Lister, she was a familiar face at the Duarte Elks Club.

Bea Cardona: Longtime Resident Recalls Duarte's Past

September 5, 2004

When Louis Cardona ventured out of Aguascalientes, Mexico, in 1918, he was searching for the good life, a life he found in Duarte. Settling into a small two-bedroom home in the section of Duarte known as Rock Town, he sent for his wife, nineteen-year-old Lupe. In that small home, the couple raised twelve children. One daughter, Bea Cardona, looks back on those days as "the happiest time of my life." Born in 1931, Bea's recollections of those days in Duarte are vivid. "We lived near the railroad tracks on Date Street," she recalls. "Nearby, there was a pig farm, the City of Hope and some old shacks that eventually burned down. There was an old lady living nearby who would pay us in Indian pennies to do her shopping for her." The nearby grocery store was on Filbert Street, a little mom-and-pop store that also sold gas.

On hot summer days, Lupe would gather her children and join other moms in the neighborhood for a trek to the San Gabriel River. The children would carry the dirty laundry, and at the river they were allowed to play in the cool waters under their mother's watchful eyes. The moms would wash the family laundry in the river and then spread a picnic on the rocky shore. "We loved Rock Town. We all got along—we didn't know we were poor," says Bea. Her father worked as a caretaker on the Woolwine Estate and for a while was employed as a gardener at the home of the famed bandleader Glenn Miller.

But the inviting river that brought so much joy would occasionally turn nasty. Bea recalls a series of floods, most particularly the flood of 1938. After days of pouring rain, the river ran rampant, breaching its shores and inundating the City of Hope and surrounding neighborhoods. Many of the men in Rock Town were employed by the ranches in the Duarte foothills, as was Bea's father, Louis. The produce trucks rescued the families from the floodwaters, transporting them to high ground. Although faced with a muddy mess, the neighborhood survived.

Construction of the Santa Fe Dam; the building of the 210 Freeway, which split apart the once-cozy neighborhood; and the destruction of ranches and homes in Rock Town to make way for an industrial park were all observed by Bea.

During her teen years, Bea would walk through orchards brimming with avocados, peaches, apricots and guavas. Turkeys, chickens, cows and pigs dotted her path. Hopping onto the electric cars at Highland and Royal Oaks, she and her friends would travel to Monrovia to shop and see a double feature. The movies cost eleven cents back then.

After raising four children of her own in Duarte, Bea now lives in La Verne. "But my heart remains in Duarte," she says, and she makes it a point to join in Duarte's community events.

Margaret Helena Viramontes: An Advocate

August 18, 2011

Throughout her life, Margaret Helena Viramontes weathered many a storm, but her passion remained resolute—it was always all about the children. According to her daughters, Lisa Oldham and JoAnn Chiles, she adopted all of Duarte's children and actively served them and their parents. According to her family, she endured many hardships and racial discrimination throughout her life, which only fueled her desire to instill cultural pride in the Duarte community. She was a tireless advocate for bilingual education.

Born on April 27, 1924, Margaret was raised by her mother, Otilia Vasquez, and her stepfather, Juan Lopez. She grew up in East Pasadena, where she was affectionately called "Chihuahuita." In 1952, she married John Viramontes and moved to Duarte, where she raised her daughters, both of whom are now teachers in the San Gabriel Valley.

Margaret worked as an instructional aid (ESL) for the Duarte Unified School District starting in 1974 and remained a dedicated employee until her retirement in 1985. However, retirement only allowed her more time to work within the community. She became the "voice" for those who were unable to communicate their needs. She was the recipient of many honors recognizing her volunteer work as an advocate for veterans and for the children of Duarte. "Margaret was a matriarch or the mother of Chicano politics in Duarte and beyond," says Duarte councilmember Phil Reyes. "She dedicated her life to social justice. It wasn't about being brown. For her, it was about ensuring that the disadvantaged, the poor and the disenfranchised had a voice and access to quality services, education and the American Dream."

Margaret was a Girl Scout leader and was active in many local organizations. In 1970, she was a member of Los Duartenos, a club serving as a link between the Mexican community and the school district to foster better relationships and positive communications. She served for many years as a member of the Community Education Council, assisted with the annual health fair, crafted children's costumes and helped organize the city's Las Posadas Celebration. She served as a community resource to the past and present superintendent of the Duarte Unified School District and was an enthusiastic member of the Andres Duarte Statue Committee. "Margaret cared deeply for this community and always tried to do the right thing for its people," says Duarte mayor pro-tem Lois Gaston.

During her final year, Margaret was able to remain in the Duarte home that she loved, cared for by her daughters and other family members, neighbors and friends. Margaret died on July 17, 2011.

Chapter 3

NATURE AND WILDLIFE

Travel along Royal Oaks Drive any evening and you will see the tree-shaded bike, pedestrian and equestrian trail busy with activity. Any day of the week, the trail is alive with bicyclists, trike riders, skateboarders, moms pushing strollers, walkers, runners, Carmelite nuns, dogs and their masters and people in groups or jaunting along solo. You might even see a llama. This trail was once the Pacific Electric right-of-way, and thanks to the vision of past city officials, it was preserved and now serves as one of the most cherished gems in our community. It runs from Buena Vista on the west short of Las Lomas on the east. Since Duarte lacks an official downtown area, this trail has sometimes been called Duarte's downtown, promoting our city's claim to be the City of Health.

Duarte is also fortunate to have trails along the San Gabriel River on its eastern border. While we blame El Niño for washed-out riverside trails and insect-breeding standing pools, we can also appreciate the rewards: a stunning crop of wildflowers, flocks of swallows lured by an abundance of flying insects and often a backdrop of snow-capped mountains.

At dusk, nighthawks appear, darting after the gnats that travel in swarms like mini twisters. Nature trails allow access along the riverbed for walkers and equestrians. The Puente Largo Bridge, built in 1907, beckons pedestrians, equestrians and bicyclists to cross the river. Originally constructed to allow the Pacific Electric cars to traverse the river, the bridge was partially undermined in the floods of 1938. It was quickly renovated with steel spans.

With the demise of the Red Cars, the bridge fell into disrepair and was blocked off. Eventually, the city received a sizeable grant from the Los Angeles County Parks and Recreation Department, and the bridge was renovated, giving walkers and bikers easy access to the bike trail that runs along the east side of the river. Traveling north, you can enter Azusa Canyon. Traveling south, hikers and bikers can access Santa Fe Dam and continue along parallel with the 605 Freeway all the way to the ocean.

Fish Canyon Falls was once accessible by a two-mile trail that winds gracefully under a canopy of oaks along the river and then up the mountainside. Hikers came from near and far to swim below the three-tiered falls and bask in its beauty. The City of Duarte maintained the trail and added interpretive signs; however, Vulcan quarry operations have blocked public access to the trail, and now hikers are only admitted by appointment.

Following are articles detailing Duarte's love for the wild and free lands on its eastern border, as well as highlights from some of the fun and exciting close encounters with local wildlife.

FISH CANYON FALLS: GRANDEUR OF NATURE ALMOST WITHIN REACH

May 6, 1998

Our river and hills have attracted many of us to this area, and soon our passion for the wilderness will be further piqued with the upcoming opening of the Fish Canyon Trail.

At a round trip of nearly nine challenging miles, this trail will not be as friendly as the Old Fish Canyon Trail, which was used until blocked by the quarry operations. I traversed the original trail in the early 1980s with three young children in tow. We marveled at the canopy of live oaks and the cool creek waters tumbling over rocks and fallen trees. We could hear the thunder of the three-tiered falls and feel the cool mist before the spectacular sight came into view: curtains of water

Previous, top: Free-flowing waters once filled the San Gabriel River, which was lined with grasslands, riparian forests and marshes, attracting water birds, fishermen and hikers. Today, the river has been channelized, and its flow depends on the actions of a dam keeper. Still, it is one of Duarte's gems.

Previous, bottom: Along the Fish Canyon Trail, signs impart important nature and history facts about the canyon. *From left to right*: Pat DeVorss, Mariellen Staller and Terri Hanks.

Over the years, Fish Canyon Falls has lured hikers from throughout the San Gabriel Valley and beyond. After the trail to the falls was blocked by the rock quarry, now Vulcan, the City of Duarte attempted to offer access by forging a trail to circumvent the quarry. However, the new trail is deemed too rigorous for most.

falling eighty feet into an emerald pool. Unfortunately, the ease of the trail at that time was also inviting to those who would rather tote a rifle than a camera. Beer cans and other trash lined the pool, and graffiti decorated rocks. Occasional sounds of rifle fire echoed through the canyon.

When the quarrying operations blocked access to the trail in 1988, I had mixed emotions. Dedicated hikers could circumvent the quarry by traversing the new steep and treacherous trail only to find that the original trail had fallen in disrepair due to erosion. But those in search of a wild party place were deterred, and the natural beauty of the area could return.

Due to public demand, hikers were eventually allowed to be escorted through the quarry to the original trailhead, but only on certain weekends by appointment at the whim of Vulcan.

Midge Dollins is just shy of her eightieth birthday. She moved to Duarte in the early 1960s and recalls standing in front of her home on Random Lane scanning the hillside with her binoculars and hoping for a glimpse of her sons, who often climbed in the local foothills. It was only a few years ago that Midge experienced the Fish Canyon Trail firsthand. "I was surprised at the magnificence of the falls," says Midge. She admits to being overconfident on her return trip. Hugging the mountain to traverse a section of trail less than a foot wide, she slipped and tumbled several feet down the cliff. With horrified fellow hikers looking on, Midge became snagged on a bush just above a sheer drop-off. "Steve Warner saved me," she says proudly.

In addition to the unique falls, hikers can find evidence of the cabins that once dotted the area. Torrential rains wiped out the encampment years ago. Only telltale foundations remain.

Note: Midge Dollins passed away on October 8, 2005.

BALD EAGLES IN DUARTE?

April 24, 1996

When my son Jenner announced that he had spied a pair of bald eagles soaring above the San Gabriel River north of the Huntington Drive overpass, I was skeptical. But when an independent sighting by Jack Collins was reported to the Los Angeles County Museum of Natural History Ornithology Department, my doubts waned.

The national bird of the United States, bald eagles have suffered over the last thirty years from loss of nesting habitat and the toxic effects of DDT and other chemicals.

Their numbers are increasing today, and a population of about twenty birds resided at Big Bear Lake this winter. According to ornithologist Kimball Garrett, the eagles fly north this time of year, and it is "certainly conceivable they stopped to feed in the San Gabriel River."

An adult bald eagle's body is entirely dark, with a white head and tail and a wingspan from six and a half to eight feet. They are sometimes confused with ospreys, which have totally white undersides. Ospreys are not common in our area but have been sighted along the river when water is plentiful and fish are present.

ONCE UPON A DUARTE STORM

February 4, 2010

Hail pelting cars. Residents evacuating their homes. Schools closed due to flooding. This isn't the Southern California I know. And yet, for

The 1907 Puente Largo Bridge, built to carry the Pacific Electric cars across the river, partially collapsed in the Great Flood of 1938. It was rebuilt with steel spans to allow the rail traffic to resume. *Courtesy of the Duarte Historical Museum.*

several days, the rain fell, sometimes at an alarming pace. And as fast as a ray of sunshine appeared, a dark sky would close in and release another deluge.

Duarte came through the recent "unsettled weather" with storm drains and catch basins performing well. But there was a time when a powerful storm ravaged Duarte and its neighboring communities. History books refer to it as the "Great Flood of 1938." In March of that year, foothill communities were assaulted by ten straight days of rain, saturating the hillsides and transforming the normally tranquil San Gabriel River into a raging torrent of debris-filled water. The Puente Largo Bridge, located a few hundred yards south of the Duarte Historical Museum in Encanto Park, partially collapsed, three of its arches buckling. Responding to rising waters, Morris and San Gabriel Dams released overflow waters that raced down spillways into the canyon, exacerbating the damage below. It is said that the course of the San Gabriel River was changed forever.

Photos of the damaged bridge show teetering wood posts that supported the electrical lines for the Pacific Electric. When the bridge was repaired, the collapsed arches were replaced by steel spans to allow rail service to resume. Later, when the electric cars ceased running, the bridge fell into disrepair. Warnings and No Trespassing signs greeted all who arrived at the bridge seeking a safe way to cross. Eventually, the City of Duarte secured grant funds, and the rebuilt Puente Largo Bridge is now a favorite crossing for bikers and walkers, allowing access to the paved trail on the river's east flank. Stubs of the wooden towers remain for historical purposes.

When Monrovian Kim Anderson displayed photos of the aftermath of the 1938 flood taken by his late grandfather, there was such a bounty of interest that the temporary Duarte Museum exhibit was made permanent and remains on display. In addition, the museum acquired a four-minute Super 8 film of the torrential waters racing down the canyon and has transferred it to a video that may be played on demand in the museum library. The original film was donated by Lois Spielman of Arcadia and was recorded by her father-in-law.

Storm basins and levies have since been constructed to protect our town from a repeat of the Great Flood, which is probably why we are able to successfully weather storms like the recent one.

BIOSWALE CONSTRUCTION UNDERWAY

October 28, 2010

Why are workers, trucks and heavy equipment concentrated around a big hole at the south end of Encanto Park behind the Duarte Historical Museum? They are creating a bioswale. This leads us to ask, "What the heck is a bioswale, what does it do, why do we need it and how much is it costing us?"

Technically, a bioswale is designed to remove silt and pollution from surface runoff water and consists of a swaled drainage course filled with native vegetation. It serves as a bio filter that treats runoff before releasing it to the watershed or storm sewer. It reportedly breaks down certain pollutants. This latest addition is only part of a bigger plan.

The project is officially dubbed the City of Duarte Encanto Nature Walk Bioswale and Outdoor Nature Classroom Project. It is funded through several grants, including a $507,990 grant from the San Gabriel and Lower Los Angeles Rivers and Mountain Conservancy (RMC). It purportedly will "open up educational and recreational opportunities for visitors to the park and the adjacent San Gabriel River."

The newly constructed bioswale at Encanto Park is designed to remove silt and pollution from surface runoff water. It serves as a bio filter, treating the runoff before releasing it to the river. The community rallied at the bioswale dedication.

According to Steve Esbenshade, Duarte engineering development manager, "the Encanto Nature Walk is destined to be one of the jewels in the regional Emerald Necklace Project." The project also calls for an interpretive display and outdoor classroom.

The changes along Encanto Parkway on the west bank of the San Gabriel River have been obvious. Years ago, in an attempt to discourage the public from entering the river area, a fence was constructed and a row of oleanders planted to block the tempting view of the river. Hikers seeking river access found strategic gaps in the fence despite posted no-trespass signs.

Recently, the philosophy has made a dramatic turnabout. Through the Emerald Necklace Project, cities were encouraged to "preserve and expand open space, habitat and recreational opportunities" along the rivers of the San Gabriel Valley. Inviting the public to hike along the riverbank and enjoy one of our most desirable natural resources was at the heart of the plan. Down came the oleanders along a stretch of Encanto Parkway, opening a panoramic vista across the riverbed to the beautiful San Gabriel Mountains. Suddenly, a whole new ambience has appeared, and except for the ugly mining scars, our river and mountains are now more intimately connected to our community.

Across from Encanto Park, a nature trail beckons to those seeking exercise, solitude and the joy of nature. The Puente Largo Bridge, which once allowed a river crossing for the electric cars, links Duarte to the bike trail on the river's east bank, which in turn offers access to the mountains and coast.

Duarteans have witnessed the grand reformation of Encanto Park. Once a field of rocks and bramble bushes, it is now an "enchanting" park.

Fish Canyon: Price of Tranquility Was High; Rewards Many

May 20, 1998

Elizabeth Hoop was seven years old when she scrambled across boulders and waded through streams to visit the primitive cabin that her father helped construct for her aunt. High in a wild canyon in the San Gabriel Mountains above Duarte and Azusa, she was a happy girl, joining other children from the area to play all day long.

The year was 1921, and Elizabeth was thrilled when her parents bought their own cabin near her aunt's where she could spend weekends with her family in the one-room structure they called Ferncliff. In those years, more than fifty-nine structures dotted the area below and above the three-tiered Fish Canyon Falls, and for decades, city folks yearning for the tranquility of nature lugged burdensome supplies two miles up the rugged canyon trail to their weekend homes. There was no electricity, no phones, not even a radio. "We cranked up the old Victrola," recalled Hoop in a 1996 DCTV interview. "We'd play cards or read."

The price of tranquility was high, but the rewards were many: a natural setting, brilliant night skies and intimate family weekends. However, these pioneers also endured hardships such as traversing the strenuous trail, lacking even simple conveniences and suffering the indignity of finding their lodges vandalized time after time. Cactus, mosquitoes, poison oak, landslides and rattlesnakes were constant companions, not to mention the deerflies, carpenter bees and ticks.

Howard and Ruth McQuigg bought their cabin in the 1920s. Their daughter Jean recalls a canyon with an abundance of wildlife: large trout, deer, a variety of frogs, mountain lions, king snakes, rattlers and ring-tailed cats.

There was one day in 1968 that would remain etched in Howard McQuigg's mind. Driving home from El Monte, where he worked, he was shocked to see giant flames racing through Fish Canyon. The disastrous fire devastated the canyon, devouring cabins and destroying acres of chaparral. When at last cabin owners were allowed to return, the McQuiggs were relieved to find that their weekend abode was spared.

For those who felt lucky that fate had smiled upon them, their relief was short-lived. The next year, heavy rains gave birth to horrendous floods that swallowed cabins, burying the structures and the contents in a rock-strewn heap at the bottom of the canyon. Only four cabins were spared.

In 1971, Maureen Bowen bought a cabin in Fish Canyon and all of its contents for $500. There she spent her weekends with her young daughters, joining the small community of cabin dwellers. The canyon was always full of day hikers or scout troops camping for the night. Her children were never without new friends in this wilderness setting. But the historical cabins that were spared by fire and flood could not survive government mandates. The owners banded together, protested and even sent a representative to Washington. But in the 1970s, land leases were not renewed, the cabin owners moved out and, eventually, the structures were "blown up."

Hikers today may find remnants of those historic cabins along the trail to the Fish Canyon Falls. A few foundations remain as a reminder of the families who abandoned the luxuries of their city homes to find serenity in Fish Canyon.

The City of Duarte has installed informational signs along the trail into Fish Canyon. In this photograph, Sierra McVey reads a trail marker. Behind her are stairs that once led to a cabin.

With bittersweet memories, some cabin owners have recorded their memories on tapes, which are stored at the Duarte Historical Museum and available for visitors to enjoy.

Duarte's Fall Colors

September 19, 2004

It occurs about this time every year, the coming of fall announcing itself in subtle fashion. I suddenly notice two yellow leaves hiding in the abundant green foliage of my liquidambar tree. And in the mornings, as I serve a handful of lettuce to Myrtle, my tortoise, I note she has taken to sleeping in, languishing in her burrow until later in the day. School is in session, and students clad in shorts and sleeveless shirts are already kicking fallen leaves on their way to class.

"Every year, we look forward to the fall colors—a mixture of reds, purples, oranges and shades of yellow," says Troy Wittenbrock, Duarte field services supervisor. "The change in color is a result of chemical processes that occur in the tree as the seasons change from summer to winter," he explains. And continuing the lesson:

> *During the summer, the leaves act as factories where the food necessary for growth is manufactured. This takes place in the cells containing chlorophyll, which gives the leaf its green color. This chemical also absorbs, from sunlight, the energy that is used in transforming carbon dioxide and water to carbohydrates such as sugars and starch.*

Unconcerned with the chemical process, most of us simply enjoy this yearly phenomenon, as the trees within our borders create a visual explosion of spectacular hues. Induced by diminishing daylight hours and falling temperatures, these trees shed tons of leaves, creating work for those compelled to rake them into piles and joy for children who use them for play.

Troy, a seventeen-year Duarte employee, has outlined a few areas in Duarte where this gift from nature may be viewed in abundance. Look for the bloom of crepe myrtle along Highland Avenue and the Chinese llame in Encanto Park. Beardslee Park displays ash trees as well as silver maple, while liquidambars explode in shades of red and orange along Melcanyon Road. Mimosa trees flourish along the bike trail and Random Lane, and tulip trees, named for their tulip-shaped leaves, line Hurstview Street with yellow.

It has been tradition for the city to plant trees as symbols of special occasions and remembrances. These special trees are donated by Arbor Nursery, which is located under the power lines on Royal Oaks Drive. "It is our way of supporting the community," says Dick Edwards, whose wife, Deborah, owns the nursery. Recently, Arbor donated a *Brachychiton acerifolius* that was planted at Beardslee Park in remembrance of 9/11. According to Dick, it is an uncommon tree that he grew and nurtured. "Now it has found a good home," he says.

LEAST BELL'S VIREO: WAITING FOR BIRD'S RETURN

March 5, 2009

Ornithologist Kimball Garrett will lead an expedition along the San Gabriel River across from Encanto Park on a Duarte Historical Society–sponsored

Twice a year, the Duarte Historical Museum sponsors birding expeditions around Encanto Park and the adjacent riverbanks. Led by Kimball Garrett, collections manager at the L.A. County Museum of Natural History, the birders have spotted as many as seventy species on a walk.

search for the least Bell's vireo (LBV) on April 19. Listed as endangered by the State of California in 1984 and by the U.S. Fish and Wildlife Service in 1986, this little bird has suffered from an altered habitat thanks to the damming and channelization of lowland streams and rivers.

The LBVs are also threatened by parasitism by brown-headed cowbirds. "Habitat protection and restoration, along with localized control of cowbirds around vireo breeding territories, have resulted in a very encouraging increase in vireo numbers," according to Garrett.

How glorious were the spreading river waters that beckoned wading birds. It was not unusual to spot two dozen egrets perched in the trees along the riverbed, appearing like white ghosts against the golden foliage. Herons, ducks and even kingfishers dotted the shore, and those who strolled along the river's edge at dusk were promised the joy of beholding the erratic flight of nighthawks and bats.

According to Garrett, Bell's vireos arrive in early April, "and most have departed by late August." It seems they like to winter in the southern half of Baja. They are named after John Graham Bell (1812–1899), who collected the first specimen in Missouri in 1843. How will we know an LBV if we see one? We can, of course, look it up in any bird guide, but according to Pete Dunne (*Pete Dunne's Essential Field Guide Companion*, 2006), the bird is a "slight, spry long-tailed, pallid, effervescent, brush-hugging gremlin in vireo's clothing…its most distinctive feature being the long animate tail."

Vireo hunters will love this moderate trek, which will hopefully produce an LBV and will most certainly result in a better understanding of the natural features of the area. Garrett is the collections manager at the Los Angeles County Museum of Natural History and has led birding expeditions to many exotic areas around the world. He is coauthor of the book *Birds of the Los Angeles Region*, as well as the Roger Tory Peterson *Guide to Warblers*.

SONG OF DUARTE'S BACKYARD BIRDS

April 30, 2009

Stroll out to the Puente Largo Bridge, the walking and cycling bridge off Encanto Parkway, and as you look out over the riverbed, you may hear a question and answer floating through the air. Let me explain!

On a recent Sunday morning, a few dozen birders gathered in Encanto Park. Thankfully, a morning breeze sifted through the canyon, although the day promised sizzling temperatures. Led by ornithologist and author Kimball Garrett, the binocular-toting group set out to see a variety of birds, but the most sought-after find was a tiny grey bird known as the least Bell's vireo (LBV), which has a place on the endangered species list.

Even before leaving the area around the museum, several bird species were spotted. Kimball focused his scope on a Cooper's hawk, which perched in an alder tree, tearing apart its catch. It cooperated long enough for everyone to get a long glimpse in the scope.

It was one of those clear days that reminded us why we moved to Duarte, and although there was little water in the riverbed, the foliage was green and dotted with yellow flowers and blooming cactus. Duarte mayor John Fasana and his wife, Kris, expressed amazement at the variety of birds spotted on the ninety-minute walk. Likewise, Bonnie Kirchner exclaimed, "I'm a convert!" She evidently had decided to become a serious birder.

Venturing out onto the bridge and looking north, Kimball called attention to the song of the LBV. "It makes a call with an upward slant, as though asking a question," he said. "And then, as if answering, it calls again with a downward slant." He then mimicked the call for the group. With ears cupped, the group stood silent, and the distinct song was heard by all. Indeed, the LBV is alive and well on Duarte's eastern border.

Among the birds observed were a red-shouldered hawk; sora rail; Lesser, Lawrence's and American goldfinches; an orange bishop; rough-winged swallows; a phainopepla; lazuli bunting; yellow-breasted chat; and a western tanager.

WHEN ANIMALS ROAMED DUARTE

March 25, 2012

Sitting around camp recently at Twin Lakes near Bridgeport, my grandson Joe suddenly jumped up and pointed behind me. "Holy Moly, it's a bear!" he exclaimed. Sure enough, only a few feet away, the cinnamon-colored bear eyed us nonchalantly. I rustled the kids into the trailer, and we watched as our visitor ambled away. I couldn't wait to get home and tell the story.

However, I got home only to discover that bear sightings had become the norm in the San Gabriel foothills. Local neighborhoods were featured on news channels and in the paper. My vacation experience was no longer of interest.

There was a time pre-1900s when grizzly bears freely roamed this area, threatened only by the hunters who flocked here for the sport. According to John Robinson in his book *The San Gabriels*, "Vaqueros…stalked and captured grizzly bears…which were then dragged into the bull ring at El Pueblo de Los Angeles to participate in the brutal bear-bull contests that were popular at the time." Who knew? The last *Urus horribilis* (brown bear) was killed in 1924.

The visitor we see today is the smaller black bear, which comes in a variety of shades from creamy white to cinnamon brown to black, according to Jim Dines, mammal collections manager at the L.A. County Museum of Natural History. It is said that these bears are descendants of a dozen or so bears that were introduced in the area from Yosemite in 1933. Mostly vegetarians, black bears are content to eat mosses, berries, nuts and grasses, but they will kill and eat insects, fish and rodents. They rarely feast on large animals. And, of course, they are scavengers as well, very much attracted to human-created garbage.

While female grizzlies weigh between 300 and 400 pounds and males anywhere from 400 to 800 pounds, our black bear friends are smaller but nonetheless a force not to mess with. The bear captured by the California Department of Fish and Game on Swiss Trails Road in Duarte recently was reported to weigh only 150 pounds.

DUARTE WATER COMPANY TAPPED SAN GABRIEL RIVER

September 29, 2012

From the Native Americans to the ranchers who settled in and around the land we now called Duarte, the life-sustaining resource that beckoned was water. Our San Gabriel River flows from the mountains, through our area and into the East Los Angeles basin before arriving at the Pacific Ocean. Once a river of great natural beauty, today many areas are lined in concrete and often appear to be waterless. Once a haven for birds, it often appears sterile and unappealing.

Today, we take for granted that when we turn on the spigot, the water will flow. We drink it, bathe in it and water our yards. Little are we concerned with the source of our water and the hardships endured by residents of the past who labored to bring the wet stuff to their living quarters.

"When in the year 1841 Andres Duarte received his grant to some sixty-five thousand acres of land in Duarte, he also received the rights to one-half the water in the San Gabriel River as it passed by his Rancho," according to the book *On the Duarte*. It is doubtful that he made much use of the river water, as there was a spring at the mouth of a canyon near his homestead. In those days, water was free. The catch? You had to fetch it. That meant digging a ditch from the river to your homestead, a project that was labor intensive and fraught with problems. Imagine dipping your drinking cup into water flowing through a ditch!

Of course, as more people settled in the area, the many ditches crossing the land became problematic, and in time, residents could see that the "water problem" was out of hand. That was when the idea of a water company blossomed.

The clear waters of the San Gabriel River have beckoned many to the area, dating back to the days of the Native Americans. When ranches were established in the area, water for drinking and irrigation was brought from the river to the ranches by way of ditches.

In the late 1860s, the problems escalated, and eventually landowners south of the Santa Fe Railroad organized a company they called the Beardslee Water Ditch Company, which became incorporated in 1881. However, in 1884, a northern group also formed a water company, which it named the Duarte Mutual Water Company.

Except for drought years, the water companies reportedly functioned well. Eventually the "Upper Company" sought underground water through wells such as one established on Royal Oaks Drive east of Vineyard Avenue. The "Lower Company" dug its first well in 1918 on South Mountain Avenue. In addition to irrigation, there grew more and more demands for pressured domestic water. This was delivered through pipelines from the wells, but the effectiveness depended on where the homestead was situated. Soon landowners questioned why two companies were needed, and after a series of negotiations, the companies merged, forming the Duarte Mutual Water Company. About this time, citrus ranches were waning, with the ranches selling off into parcels, and more and more homes being built required pressured water.

In about 1950, the Public Utilities Commission was formed. Duarte's population had exploded, and the demand for irrigation water waned. New reservoirs were constructed and miles of new pipe laid. After several changes in the water company ownerships, the California-American Water Company took over, and it remains in charge today. The water that flows from your faucet comes from groundwater sources from the main San Gabriel Basin. Its journey was a long, hard one that began in the most primitive of methods and developed over the years to the modern system that thus far is reliable and safe. I'll drink to that!

ROAD OPENS ACCESS TO CRYSTAL LAKE

May 2011

It was a fine spring day as we negotiated sharp curves up the canyon. Steep crumbling cliffs, sparkling lakes and stalks of colorful wildflowers marked the way. Arriving at the end of the road, I stepped out of the car, turning my face to the sun, which warmed the air despite a chilled breeze wafting across scattered mounds of snow. The scent of fresh pine was exhilarating. It was hard to believe that we were not in the High Sierras but merely in the San Gabriel Mountains' Azusa Canyon, only about forty-five minutes from home.

Celebrating the fact that Highway 39 to Crystal Lake recently opened after having been closed since the Curve fire in 2002, we planned on having lunch at the Crystal Lake Snack Bar and Store, simply referred to as the Crystal Lake Café. Only a few cars were parked in the lot, and when we arrived, café owner Adam Samrah rushed out to greet us. "It has been pretty lonely up here," admitted Samrah. Since 2002, he and his wife, Rula, and their sons A.J and Zachary have resided in a cabin behind the café, pretty much exiled from civilization. Occasionally, Samrah would take his sons to the West Covina Mall to play with other children. Except for a few bicyclists, visitors to their cabin since the road closure have been of the four-legged variety: deer, bear, coyotes, mountain lions, bobcats "and a ton of squirrels."

With the road in use, life has changed. Samrah now enjoys cooking the special items on the café's menu, with help from his wife, who fills the demand for her coveted banana nut bread and fudge. "Return patrons sit on the steps and enjoy the aroma as they patiently wait for the bread and fudge to emerge from the oven," laughs Samrah. Having worked for years as

The Crystal Lake Café serves campers and day visitors in the canyon above Azusa. Adam Samrah is always on hand to greet patrons. His life in the canyon is rewarding, although there have been close calls with fires, floods and road closures.

a French chef, Samrah incorporates that flair into his menu. A favorite is his charbroiled chicken sandwich with aioli sauce. "I cook fresh chicken breasts that I have marinated in wine," says Samrah. "I don't use processed lunch meat." His chili and breakfast burritos are also popular.

Gleeful that the open road now offers access to motorists, Samrah says he meets people from all over the world who drive up the canyon and stop at the café. He opens early for breakfast and remains available until the dinner patrons leave, usually around 7:00 p.m. But true to his easygoing personality, he is always willing to remain open later if the demand is there.

The road at this time ends at the café, about 5,800 feet in elevation. Visiting the lake and the campground, at which renovation is not yet completed, involves a short hike. Although the campground is scheduled to open for the summer, such has not been officially announced. When the lake and campground are accessible by car, Samrah expects a flood of customers and will finally be in his element. At that time, he will stock the snack bar for the campers and day hikers.

Although the Samrah family looks forward to more visitors, they have enjoyed living in the canyon even through the lonely years. "I love living up here," says Samrah. "I don't want to live anywhere else. I'll die here."

Note: In July 2012, we made another visit to the Crystal Lake Camp Store to catch up on the progress. The campground is renovated, and the primitive sites are shaded by a canopy of stately oaks. At the Crystal Lake Snack Bar and Trading Post, Samrah greeted us warmly and plied us with fresh banana bread and brownies. He became rather famous in 2002 when the Curve fire drove him and a friend racing through its wake. His friend's cabin burned to the ground while the two men huddled in a pond surrounded by fire, narrowly escaping death. One week after our visit, the Williams fire broke out in the San Gabriel Canyon. Although the fire raged northeast of Crystal Lake, there were evacuations ordered. Samrah delivered his family safely to his second home down the mountain and then returned to protect his store. He had stocked it with everything needed to serve the Labor Day weekend crowd only to find himself alone. Such is the life of a mountain man.

CONDORS OVER DUARTE?

April 3, 2008

"I know this sounds unbelievable," the voice-mail message began, "but there is a gigantic black bird circling over the Mesa, and I think...excuse me if this is silly, but I think it is a condor!" I smiled as I listened, because this wasn't the first time a resident has inquired as to whether condors visit our local air space.

Some people mistakenly think of me as a birding expert, but I was not blessed with the skillful birder genes possessed by my brother, ornithologist Kimball Garrett. Therefore, when bird questions come my way, an immediate call or e-mail to Kimball at the L.A. County Museum of Natural History gets me an answer.

Ten thousand years ago, the condor range spread over most of North America. Living along the grassy banks of the waterway we call the San Gabriel River, Native Americans revered the condors, incorporating them into their religious rituals. However, because these magnificent birds require vast areas of remote wilderness for foraging, roosting and nesting, urban sprawl has nearly caused their undoing. "In the early 1900s, there were some well-known condor nests in the Mount Wilson area," says Kimball. "And prior to that, condors certainly would have ranged all along the south front of the San Gabriels, including the Duarte area." But not recently. By 1940, their range was reduced to the coastal mountains of Southern California, their numbers dwindling, and it wasn't until a concerted effort was launched to capture and then reintroduce these birds back into the wild that they began a comeback.

Will they appear again in Duarte? "I guess that depends on how recovery efforts go," says Kimball. We can all help that day arrive by mitigating some of the human-caused obstacles, such as banning the use of lead bullets (recently made law by the California legislature), cleaning up roadside trash, properly disposing of such hazardous materials as antifreeze and curbing over-development.

The recent condor sighting came from Coach Rodney Jefferson, a 1978 Duarte High School graduate. He is the founder and director of "A" Game Fundamentals Basketball Clinic, a program for boys and girls from fifth to eleventh grades living in Monrovia and Duarte. My advice was, "Get out your binoculars and bird identification guide" and take another look.

What a spectacular sight to see—huge ruffled wings gracefully soaring on the wind currents in spiral fashion. But in most cases, the celebrated bird is not the condor but the turkey vulture, affectionately called "TV" in the birding world.

ARTIFACTS SHED LIGHT ON ANCIENT LOCAL HISTORY

September 3, 2006

There once was a wild and natural river flowing from tributaries high in the mountains to deliver the gift of pristine waters to the people of the valley below. That river, once sacred and life sustaining to the Native Americans, is treated with much disrespect today. The San Gabriel River on Duarte's eastern border has been channelized, regulated by a dam, clogged with nonnative vegetation and trashed during the summer months. And yet, in contrast to the cement and asphalt that dominate the city, a walk along the river's edge offers a sweet taste of wilderness.

Archaeologists recently discovered a milling area estimated to be eight thousand years old at the base of the San Gabriel Mountains on the east flank of the river, offering a glimpse into prehistoric times. According to an article in *USA Today*, archaeologists have known since the 1960s that the area once contained artifacts, "but the exact location of the milling site was not discovered until this year." The site was discovered on land previously occupied by the Monrovia Nursery and has yielded large arrowheads, hearths and stone slabs used to grind seeds and acorns.

The Native Americans who lived peacefully at the river's edge were the Tongva people, meaning "people of the earth" in the Tongva language. In modern times, they are often referred to as the Gabrielinos, following the Spanish custom of naming local tribes after nearby missions. The artifacts indicate that the excavated area was a camp used to process "abundant local plant materials, including oak, California black walnut, prickly pear cactus, holly and yucca, all of which are still present in the area."

Saddened by the fact that we have disturbed the ancient history of our local area, Suzanne Avila, vice-president of the Azusa Historical Society and founder of the Think River Watershed Education Program, feels that now that the artifacts have been unearthed, it is incumbent upon us to learn from them and be reminded that the river is not ours. "We must respect the river as our life-giving source and realize that we are a part of nature," she says.

In an effort to honor the prehistoric Tongva archaeological finds, the Azusa Historical Society and the Duarte Historical Society are jointly inviting the public to join in *Somos del Rio* ("We Are the River"), a blessing of the San Gabriel River and an "appreciation of all things natural." The blessing will be conducted by a member of the Gabrielino Tongva Tribal

Council, followed by a lecture on historic life along the San Gabriel River by U.S. Forest Service naturalist Steve Segreto. Focus will be placed on the village of Ashuukshanga, precursor to the present-day city of Azusa.

MESA IS PEACEFUL BUT FIRE PRONE

November 29, 2007

Whether banding together for protection from marauding bears or planning a reception party for a herd of turf-devouring goats, Duarteans who reside on the mesa above town are special folks. Composed of some ninety-five homes, this neighborhood is known for its dedicated and hardworking volunteers who serve our community. They live in one of Duarte's most unique areas, commonly referred to as the Duarte Mesa.

Bill and Nita Norgard built their home on the Mesa in 1972. "The area was originally owned by the Spinks family," says Bill. "There was an avocado orchard and a reservoir at the north end of Spinks Canyon Road." The Norgards found proof of this historical fact when they uncovered concrete and galvanized pipes for the orchard when they broke ground to build. The Norgards are a good example of a community-minded family. And if there is a fundraising effort in town for the Friends of the Library or the Duarte Education Foundation, you can bet they are on the committee.

The Mesa is a unique and peaceful place, offering spectacular views of the valley. However, it is also a fire-prone area. Following the 1980 fire that destroyed many Mesa homes, the residents formed the Duarte Mesa Association, a voluntary organization that at that time helped fire victims rebuild. Today, the association flourishes in many ways, giving opportunity to these close-knit neighbors to share ideas on how to coexist with wildlife, protect their homes from fires and promote neighborhood watch activities.

"When I first moved to California," says Carie Osburn, a Mesa resident since 1987, "I lived in Santa Monica, where I met only two neighbors in seven years." Today, Carie is pleased to say, "What makes the Mesa so special to me is that I know almost every family out of the one hundred homes on the Mesa." She mirrors the sentiments of many Mesa residents when she says that she is impressed with the residents' community spirit, a fact that became evident at a block party honoring Mesa residents who give back to the community. The list, says Carie, was impressive and included volunteer hours for the Duarte mentoring program, SAT and ACT training, Friends of the Library, school and college boards, public safety and the Duarte Museum, to mention a few.

Recently, Mesa residents held a reception to greet a herd of goats hired by the city to clear brush on the hillsides.

"D" BRANDING IRON GETS AN F

March 31, 2011

It is a familiar letter to residents of Duarte, displayed on the mountainside, on city signs in the parks and median and on stationery and local publications. It is the very unique lowercase letter "d" that, in a stylized way, represents the original "d" registered in 1843 by our town's namesake, Andres Avelino Duarte.

On display at Duarte City Hall is purportedly the "original" branding iron of Señor Duarte, but that claim is now facing scrutiny. "The branding iron exhibited at City Hall was clearly made by arc welding, so it cannot be a Mexican-period branding iron. That could only have been produced by a blacksmith," says Irwin Margiloff, curator of the Duarte Historical Museum.

No one knows just where or when branding originated, but it can be proven that branding was done at least two thousand years before Christ. Tombs in Egypt have pictures of the actual work of branding animals.

Cattle ranching was introduced in California in 1769. Franciscan priests traveling with the Portola expedition brought with them cattle for dairy and breeding purposes. The first cattle to roam the area that would become the Rancho Santa Anita were from the Mission San Gabriel herd, which at one time numbered as many as twenty-six thousand head.

In the late 1700s, it became popular for retiring soldiers to remain locally rather than return to their homelands. Many received sizable land grants, a practice that continued after Mexico won its independence from Spain. By the 1840s, many ranchos existed. With no fences to corral the cattle, branding became necessary to identify stock. As a mark of identification, the brand is perfect, although the animal might disagree. It is applied in a moment yet remains as long as the animal lives. Within each state in the United States, a brand may be used only once. Permission by the owner must be granted before a brand may be copied.

The original "d" brand registered in 1843 by our town's namesake, Andres Avelino Duarte, is now a city symbol and used on signs and stationery. There is somewhat of a controversy over where the original iron is located.

While researching the whereabouts of the original branding iron of the Duarte Rancho, the Duarte Museum was contacted by Manuel Alberto Duarte of Llano, Texas. He is a great-great-grandson of Andres Duarte and claims to be in possession of the original branding iron of Felipe Duarte, Andres's only son, and has furnished a photo of the tool in question. "What is striking," says Margiloff, "is how different it is from the form that was registered in 1843. The original registry entry is located in the L.A. County Natural History Museum's Seaver Collection and was written by the registrar with a pen, making it appear simpler than the rounded version appearing on the hill overlooking the city. The original form was a lowercase 'd' with a tilde as the top serif and an arrowhead on the extension of the lower serif, while the brand in the possession of Manuel Alberto Duarte is in the form of a capital 'D' with a simplified tilde and a straight-line extension rather than an arrowhead." Margiloff has personally examined the drawing in the Seaver Collection.

The investigation, according to Margiloff, "gets more interesting as time goes on." He would like to employ the PBS History Detectives to undertake an examination of Felipe's branding iron, and if such cannot be arranged, "we can perhaps locate a historically minded blacksmith and/or an expert in metallurgy to authenticate it—or not!"

NEW BOOK HIGHLIGHTS DUARTE'S HILLSIDE "D"

September 6, 2007

Across the nation, hillside letters dot the landscape. Do they represent city pride, wanton graffiti, adherence to tradition? A recently released book entitled *Hillside Letters A–Z* traces the history of these prominent monograms, their roots, meanings, construction and appearance. The Duarte "d" emblazoned on the hillside above our town rates special mention in this publication, and rightfully so. Duarte's "d" represents the brand of our city's namesake, Andres Avelino Duarte, making it one of the most unique and meaningful letters to grace a town.

The saga behind Duarte's "d," although not without controversy, pales in comparison to that of Cal State Berkeley's "Big C." Erected in 1905, it has, through the years, been subjected to numerous attacks by rivals, some of which escalated into violence, rendering the hillside a "battleground." The book details some of the pranks and states that today the once-famous letter hides behind "overgrown eucalyptus and Monterey pines."

Duarte's "d" is arguably our city's first piece of public art. Built in 1979, it was originally crafted from vegetation outlined with concrete. In 1988, the vegetation was replaced by concrete, alleviating the need for constant maintenance. The sign was originally wired for lighting that would have illuminated the monogram during the evenings so that its soft glow could be seen from the 210 Freeway. But this lovely display was short-lived, as a few residents complained that the lighting interfered with their stargazing. Troy Wittenbrock, field services supervisor, says that a city crew treks up the hill through dry brush and poison oak to repaint the green-and-white letter about once every five years.

Describing Duarte's "d," the book features a photo of the monogram and the branding iron. It states in part: "Most hillside emblems are simple block letters that represent the name of a school or community, but the 'd' that overlooks the community of Duarte, California, a few miles east of

A newly released book features hillside letters that mark many communities in the nation. Duarte's "d" is one of the letters featured in the book. Our hillside "d" is a stylized insignia of great historical significance.

Pasadena, is a stylized insignia of great historical significance." It goes on to recite a short account of Andres Duarte's life and recognizes the prominent role that the branding iron "d" plays in our town today.

The book claims that the first hillside letter appeared in March 1905, "a sixty-foot-tall concrete 'C' on Charter Hill overlooking the San Francisco Bay," and that although letters appear on hillsides all over the nation, they are "primarily a phenomenon of the American West, where there are vast landscapes of treeless hillsides visible for miles." It continues, "The tradition was most popular before the rise of environmentalism and the growing aesthetic preference for untouched natural landscapes."

Author Evelyn Corning, who lives in Tucson, Arizona, visited Duarte while writing her book. "I was impressed with the uniqueness of your letter," she writes. "It is a fine example of an enduring landmark, a source of pride and unity to the people of your community."

THE SEQUENT OCCUPANCE OF THE RANCHO AZUSA DE DUARTE

January 25, 2007

Tree crops dominate the cultivated land, and citrus trees dominate its orchard patterns. Avocado trees are widely scattered, small relict orchards of English walnut trees are notable and small persimmon orchards dot the landscape. Winter grain is grown on the foothill mesas where soil is too shallow for tree crops and streets for residential subdivisions invade the fields. Patches of irrigated field crops, chiefly alfalfa, remain in the southwest, but they too are shrinking as residential occupance spread.

These descriptions, which give us a unique glimpse into Duarte's history, are offered in a book with a complicated title: *The Sequent Occupance of the Rancho Azusa de Duarte: A Segment of the Upper San Gabriel Valley of California.* This detailed historical account has been lauded as the most authoritative, complete work ever written on the old rancho from the standpoint of the people and their agricultural occupancy. According to *On the Duarte*, much of the research relied on when the former book was written is no longer available. But who would take the time and painstaking research to write such a book?

In 1884, the Reverend David Shaw Shrode, a blacksmith and wagonmaker, crafted the wagon that brought his family west to Duarte. He was a lay minister in the Southern Methodist Church and, until his death in 1895, served as the superintendent of the Sunday school, which first met in the Duarte Elementary School House. The reverend's eldest son, affectionately known as Jake, married Mary Patterson in 1884, and the couple raised three daughters. It was his daughter Ida May who is responsible for the book in question.

Dr. Ida May Shrode became an instructor at Pasadena City College and, like her father, served as an officer and director of the Beardslee Water Ditch Company and on the Fruit Exchange Board. She lived in the home in which she was born on South California Avenue until she sold the land in 1949. Ida May's contribution to the written history of Duarte was her doctoral dissertation, which was submitted to the faculty of the Division of Physical Science, Department of Geography, University of Chicago.

It is her descriptions of the land that bring our history to life, allowing one to picture the landscape and daily life of early Duarte. Some of the words she used seem odd today. She describes the "Glendora-Monrovia Line of the Pacific Electric Railway," which provided transportation to and from Los Angeles, and the main line of the Atchison, Topeka and Santa Fe along the north side of Duarte Road. There was the Monrovia Airport on the south of Highway 66, which served as an emergency landing field for private planes. Duarte was home to hog ranches, chicken farms and "acres of pigeon raising and squab selling." On the commercial side, May describes the "restaurants, cocktail bars, novelty shops, service stations, nursery sales yards and other vending establishments which face the heavy traffic."

Tracing Duarte's history from the time of Don Andres Duarte until the publishing of her book, Dr. May's concerns are not that much different from those we face today: the use of the land, access to clean and healthy water for the population and crops and a healthy balance between industry and residential areas.

Chapter 4

ORGANIZATIONS

THERE IS A CLUB FOR JUST ABOUT EVERYONE IN DUARTE

February 10, 1999

During their child-rearing years, many Duarte women became involved in PTAs or parenting organizations. But where do women find female companionship and community ties after the last child leaves home? Locally, there are many social- and service-oriented clubs, many geared toward membership of women in the workplace. Following are a few.

The Emblem Club: A national organization, this club is the woman's counterpart to the Elks and boasts a membership of more than one hundred women from the area.

The Rotary Club: There was a day when women were not welcomed into the folds of the Rotary Club, but the Duarte Rotary changed all that. The local chapter was expelled from the national organization but later rejoined after a Supreme Court ruling dictated that the national club change its policy to allow female members

Duarte Woman's Club: In a quest to promote friendship, the sharing of ideas and community service, this club admits women over the age of eighteen. The monthly evening meetings held at the Duarte Community

Center allow both working and non-working women to remain active in the club.

Duarte Reading Circle: Founded in 1909, this club consists of an intimate group of women who take turns hosting meetings in their homes. Their prime objective is to read together, share books and promote reading in the community.

Most contemporary local clubs have dropped any restrictions as far as the sex of participants.

The Kiwanis: This organization is dedicated to changing the world, one child and one community at a time. Our local Kiwanis Club is extremely active in serving the community and our students.

Toastmasters: Improving communication skills for work or self-improvement is the goal of this club.

Rancho de Duarte Garden Club: Promoting the improvement of the environment through gardening is a prime goal of this club. Members host shows to display their green-thumb talents.

Duarte Historical Society: This club manages the Duarte Historical Museum and is dedicated to sharing and preserving local history through talks, displays and its newsletter, *The Branding Iron*.

Note: This article only covers a few of our local clubs. There are many more active social and philanthropic organizations in town. More clubs have sprouted since the article was written, while some mentioned have since disbanded.

Continuing the Reading Circle

March 2009

The group may be a bit more "hip," and perhaps the refreshments from time to time may call for ditching the tea and partaking in a glass of champagne, but the core value of Duarte's New Reading Circle will remain true to the stated purpose of the original circle that formed on April 6, 1909: "The purpose of the Circle shall be to promote interest in reading good literature and to create sociability in the community."

It was a century ago this week that seventeen Duarte ladies gathered to form their circle, declaring a limit of thirty members and assessing dues of five cents per member per month. A special book was chosen to be read at each meeting, the first of which was *Aunt Jane from Kentucky*.

As I perused the list of ladies who formed the original circle, I couldn't help but notice that many were the same names so prominent in Duarte's history: Beardslee, Fowler, Shrode, Abouchar, Maxwell and Blaine, to name a few. Because the ladies held the meetings in their homes, they felt it was not proper to invite gentlemen to join the club. Today's New Reading Circle will limit membership not by sex but by one's interest in the written word.

After seventy-five years in existence, the first Reading Circle remained strong, with the members not only pursuing their interest in reading and sharing current events but also participating in fundraisers donating to a variety of charities.

Only recently, and on the cusp of their 100th anniversary, the club, down to only a few members, most in their eighties, chose to disband. Historical records were turned over to UCLA and the Duarte Historical Museum.

However, for the past several years, another dedicated group of readers has banded together to promote reading in our community. These readers are the hardworking individuals who make up the Friends of the Library and those who formed the committee that graces our town with the impressive Festival of Authors, an annual event envied by neighboring communities.

Gathering recently, four community members—Mary Barrow Somerlott, Pat De Rose, Kathy Kirchner and Nita Norgard—drafted the beginnings of the New Reading Circle, declaring that membership shall be "open to anyone with an interest."

Elks Settle in Duarte, Constructing Clubhouse

January 12, 2003

Duarte is a town of people with big hearts. With a relatively small population, our city still boasts an abundance of civic organizations, hardworking volunteers, clubs dedicated to helping others and an outreach center open to anyone who needs assistance. And so, with open arms, we welcome the Duarte Elks Club, an organization dedicated to raising money for charity.

Originally named the Monrovia Elks Club, this group formed in 1922 and built a lodge on Foothill Boulevard in Monrovia in the early 1930s. For years, the club flourished, raising money for charity and offering its facilities for hundreds of local events. When the membership began to dwindle, it was no longer financially feasible to maintain the building, so it was sold and the money used to build a new lodge in Duarte.

Traveling on Huntington Drive east of Mount Olive, we have witnessed an area on the south side of the street being cleared and sitting idle for years. Finally, during the last several months, we have watched with curiosity as a building has been under construction.

After negotiating scores of obstacles, a home for the Duarte Elks is imminent, and the membership of about two hundred members, mainly from Sierra Madre, Monrovia and Duarte, looks forward to an anticipated opening in March. The building will fit in with the architecture along Huntington Drive and offer plenty of parking.

The Duarte Elks is affiliated with the San Gabriel Valley District and State Elks and the National Grand Lodge headquartered in Chicago.

Chapter 5

SCHOOLS

The Monrovia-Duarte Black Alumni Association Honors Its Own

September 13, 2012

The economy may be down, but Duarte is rich—in diversity that is. Our local history is flush with stories about a variety of ethnic groups that have contributed greatly to our present quality of life. The Duarte Historical Museum will offer a detailed exhibit on our local black history presented by the Monrovia-Duarte Black Alumni Association.

The exhibit, largely organized by Eloise Hart, has mainly focused on Monrovians. However, with the help of our local museum, it will now include several Duarteans. With community input, more may be added.

When Don and Bernice Watson sought to buy a home in Duarte's Fish Canyon, they knew it would be an uphill battle, given the racial climate at the time. But buy a home they did, and in an era when such was a difficult task for minorities. As time went on, both earned their place in Duarte history. Don was elected mayor of Duarte in 1971, becoming the first black mayor in the San Gabriel Valley. He was again elected mayor in 1974. Bernice at one time served as a publicist for the Duarte School District and is perhaps best known as coauthor of *On the Duarte*, a comprehensive history of Duarte during its formative years.

Another outstanding black Duartean is Dr. Sylvia Whitlock, the first woman in the world to serve as president of a Rotary Club. She was at the heart of the Duarte Rotary Supreme Court victory, which opened the doors to women in service clubs.

Douglas Ross, still active in community affairs, was raised in Duarte in what was once known as Rock Town. Memories of life in Duarte during the 1950s and '60s remain vivid to him, and it is his hope to memorialize that part of Duarte's history in a book.

We are fortunate to have Everett Adams living in Duarte today. His childhood memories are like a historical novel as he tells tales of his family's adventures on the Baird Ranch during the 1930s and '40s.

Other outstanding black Duarteans include Lela Wallace, who spent most of her thirty-five-year teaching career at Valley View School; Ron Husband, who achieved success as a talented illustrator and animator for Walt Disney; Hardiman Cureton, who was named to *Look* magazine's "All American Football Team" in 1955; and, of course, those who currently play major roles in today's community, such as former mayor Lois Gaston and longtime school board member Ken Bell.

GERI WHITELEY HOULIHAN: A DUARTE HIGH REUNION

September 14, 2011

As the years pass, some memories fade, while others linger, poised to resurface at the slightest nudge. For Geri Whiteley (now Houlihan), the thrill of becoming the first homecoming queen of the newly built Duarte High School is one such memory.

"It all started in 1957," she recalls, "when a brand-new high school was being built for Duarte. The graduates from three grammar schools—Northview, Royal Oaks and Andres Duarte—were slated to be the first students. A new school just for us!"

Anticipation grew, only to be dashed when it was announced that the new school was behind schedule and would not be completed on time. The disappointed students attended Monrovia-Arcadia-Duarte (MAD) High School for three months.

When the new school finally opened, the students found "new" to be the operative word. In addition to the new facilities, the students tackled such tasks as creating clubs and traditions, many of which endure today. "Our job was to come up with school colors, mascot, song and rules," says Geri. "We chose turquoise and white for colors, the Falcon for our mascot and elected a student council. We even composed and sang the alma mater."

The first student government, which was also referred to as a "steering committee," was formed of two students from each grammar school: Mike Chase and Ricky Swain from Royal Oaks, Margie Perkins and Buddy Reich from Northview and Geri Whiteley and Barbara Ridgeway from Andres Duarte. For the next four years, Robert Manning was the principal.

Other organizations and traditions also began, including the Girls Athletic Association, Block D, Dals, the Falconettes, the school band and the school newspaper, *The Falconeer*. The glee clubs, yearbook, song leaders, majorettes, flag twirlers and various sports teams were also formed.

It was a busy time for DHS's first students. Except for all the work involved in creating a foundation for those who would follow, the next four years were typical high school. "We were a close-knit group, like brothers and sisters. We had school dances, broke hearts, went steady and wore our letterman jackets. Oh, and we studied!" says Geri.

In 1961, the time for graduation of the first students at DHS had arrived, and the school's first Hall of Fame recipients were named:

Best All Around: Diane Laban and Larry Shelton
Best Personality: Carol Nostrame and Buddy Reich
Best Sense of Humor: Kelly Larson and Ed Cartwright
Best Spirit: Jan Bullington and Robert Byerly
Friendliest: Doreen Donaldson and Jim McClung
Best Looking: Margie Perkins and Kent Winkler
Most Athletic: Donna Parent and Daryl Mead
Walking Encyclopedias: Valeda Quincy and Dennis Cruise

Geri now resides in Glendora and is retired. Having savored those special days throughout the years, the Duarte High School class of 1961 will reunite on September 24.

CHEF RICE AND THE CULINARY ARTS

December 27, 2012

Louis Rice faced the biggest challenge of his life when he accepted an instructor position at Duarte High School to teach the ROP culinary arts class. He was armed with the virtues he possessed to be a successful chef: toughness, focus and directness. It wasn't long before he learned that these attributes didn't work with students. "I had to become vulnerable," he says. "I quickly learned to adjust and let my students see me as a person. It changed my life." He sees this as the key to his success as a teacher.

Always pursuing his goal to be an executive chef, Chef Rice now enjoys his life as an instructor, not only teaching his students the basic skills of cooking but also preparing them for entry-level positions in commercial kitchens or trade school. His goal is to connect students with their passion for cooking and provide them with the skills they will need. He confesses that the skills he strives to teach are not just how to bake a pie but more important skills in the workplace today such as good hygiene, promptness, a strong work ethic, honor, integrity, perseverance, leadership and commitment. These skills he sees as prime ingredients for a successful person in whatever field they enter.

While some ROP culinary arts students just want to learn to cook, others yearn for a career as a chef or baker. The classes consist of about 65 percent girls. The chief goal is to learn to operate a business, but cooking basics are also stressed, including food safety, sanitation, recipe conversions, knife cuts, stocks and sauces and marinades. When asked who pays for the groceries, Chef Rice admits that he fronts the money and is reimbursed by the class fundraisers, which consist of catering events. "That is the way it works, and I'm happy to do it," he says.

I met Chef Rice and his "crew" as they dished up food to the VIPs attending a dinner before the Duarte High School homecoming game and dedication of the school's new sports field. They have catered events for as many as three hundred people. To prepare the food, they operate like a commercial kitchen, each of the six classes taking a "shift" and a level of responsibility. If they don't finish, the work goes to the next class.

The students have catered events for the football team and school district and once prepared a pasta dinner as a fundraiser to help pay for services for a student's father's burial expense. A favorite event was preparing a meal for a crew working on a home for Habitat for Humanity. Their signature dish is what they call "Chocolate Symphony," a brownie that contains the main ingredients of "tender love and care" mixed in with a lot of chocolate and caramel sauce.

Chef Rice teaches six classes a week, seemingly a full-time job, but he also works as a chef for special events at the Long Beach Convention Center and the Aquarium of the Pacific. And he recently took on another client, the USS *Iowa*.

Through his contacts, he aims to help his students who aspire to chefdom to find work in the culinary field. One student, only sixteen years old, is very passionate about becoming a chef and with Chef Rice's help has landed an internship at the Pasadena Baking Company later this year.

Chef Rice and his students were recognized for their achievements at the Duarte City Council meeting on December 11.

CONCLUSION

In many ways, the city of Duarte is much like other San Gabriel foothill communities flavored with a dash of uniqueness. Its citizens represent dozens of ethnic backgrounds melded together in harmony. The racial tensions of the 1960s have subsided, and everywhere in Duarte—from the schools to the shops to the parks—variety is the norm.

We are lucky to have a caring city staff and city council. Their prudence has kept us sound fiscally. Sure, we have had to give up services and vote in bond issues to keep afloat, but here we are, still standing! Our town's agenda is a positive one, marred only by a few issues, which we are working on.

For years, a group of Duarteans has insisted that Duarte create a town center, and the feasibility of such a goal has resulted in studies and committees, with no success so far. Another issue is the ongoing insistence of Azusa, our neighbor to the east, to allow Vulcan to relocate its quarry operations to the mountain behind Duarte, relieving Azusa of the unsightly gouging of the hillside and shifting the mess to our backyard. One would think that the border between Duarte and Azusa would be the San Gabriel River, but such is not the case. The border is skewed so that the hillside area behind Duarte's Fish Canyon homes is within the Azusa boundary line. Naturally, Duarteans are against quarry operations in their backyards, which will not only be unsightly but will also create noise, dust and a host of health issues. Azusa, on the other hand, will continue to benefit from the revenue that the quarry brings it while Duarte suffers. The matter is in the hands of the courts and has cost the City of Duarte funds it would have rather spent on needed services. To me, the issue is not a legal one but an affront to the Golden Rule and a basic good-neighbor policy.

A small-town atmosphere, dozens of ethnic eateries, large and small shops and grocery stores and a multitude of parks and hiking trails grace our town. Our neighborhoods band together under the neighborhood watch program. Our students enjoy safe schools with caring staffs. Our town recently dedicated a new sports field at the high school, and our students have every opportunity to succeed in academic life. Our city council members and city staff meld with the community as friends and equals, not an untouchable ruling body.

Our small-town atmosphere is celebrated with such events as the annual Salute to Route 66 Parade and City Picnic, as well as the placement of a fourteen-foot-tall bronzed statue of our namesake, Andres Avelino Duarte, which sits on Huntington Drive across from City Hall, where he keeps vigil over the town. Although the city helps in many ways, projects such as the parade and statue were conceived and largely executed by grassroots groups of residents.

Duarte's population is approximately twenty-two thousand residents. We are, in a sense, an island. To our north loom the lovely San Gabriel Mountains; to our east, the San Gabriel River; to the south, the quarry pits; and our good neighbor Monrovia to the west. With easy access to the 605 and 210 Freeways, travel is convenient whether headed to the ocean, the Inland Empire or Los Angeles.

For all these reasons and many more, Duarte is "Our Kind of Town."

ABOUT THE AUTHORS

Claudia Heller

The eldest of seven children, Claudia grew up in Hollywood, California, and graduated from Los Angeles City College with a degree in journalism. Living in Duarte for the past thirty years, she has served as president of the Duarte Historical Society and Museum for the past fifteen years. She writes a bimonthly column for the *Star News*, an insert in the *Pasadena Star News*. Her columns cover people, events and history of the Duarte area. She is the author of *Life on Route 66: Personal Accounts Along the Mother Road to California*. She is retired from her career in the legal field.

Alan Heller

Growing up in Silverlake, California, Alan earned a BA in biology at California State University, Los Angeles. He currently serves as president of Duarte's Public Access Channel (DCTV) and is a former commissioner of the Duarte Parks and Recreation Commission, the Duarte Planning Commission and the Duarte Community Service Commission. Alan is a member of the Los Angeles Westerners Corral of History Writers and the

Ancient and Honorable Order of E Clampus Vitus, a "disorganization" that places history plaques throughout the West. He is coauthor of *Life on Route 66: Personal Accounts Along the Mother Road to California*, having provided the book's photos.

ALAN AND CLAUDIA HELLER

Married for forty-nine years, the couple raised three children in Duarte and are today enjoying their five grandchildren. As a family, they enjoyed many years of camping throughout the United States. Since retiring in 2010, they purchased an eighteen-foot trailer and enjoy exploring the western United States, especially the Southwest, the Eastern Sierras and the National Mojave Preserve. They are members of the Desert Explorers and Friends of the Old Mojave Road. In 2010, they spent two months traveling Route 66 to Chicago, writing a series of articles for the San Gabriel Valley Newspaper Group. Those articles and photos were combined in a book entitled *Life on Route 66: Personal Accounts Along the Mother Road to California*, which was published in June 2012.

Photographer Alan Heller and author Claudia Heller.